THE CATHOLIC BISHOPS AND
NUCLEAR WAR

A CRITIQUE AND ANALYSIS OF THE PASTORAL
THE CHALLENGE OF PEACE

THE CATHOLIC BISHOPS AND
NUCLEAR WAR

A CRITIQUE AND ANALYSIS
OF THE PASTORAL
THE CHALLENGE OF PEACE

JUDITH A. DWYER, S.S.J.,
Editor

GEORGETOWN UNIVERSITY PRESS
Washington, D.C.

Copyright © 1984 by Georgetown University Press

All Rights Reserved

Printed in the United States of America

Library of Congress Cataloging in Publication Data

Main entry under title:

The Catholic bishops and nuclear war.

    1. Catholic Church. National Conference of Catholic
Bishops. Challenge of peace—Addresses, essays,
lectures. 2. Atomic warfare—Religious aspects—
Catholic Church—Addresses, essays, lectures.
3. Peace—Religious aspects—Catholic Church—Addresses,
essays, lectures. 4. Catholic Church—United States—
Pastoral letters and charges—Addresses, essays,
lectures. 5. Catholic Church—Doctrines—Addresses,
essays, lectures. I. Dwyer, Judith A. II. Catholic
Church. National Conference of Catholic Bishops. The
challenge of peace.

BX1795.A85C39 1983 Suppl. 4   261.8'73   84-4006
ISBN 0-87840-409-0

CONTENTS

Preface

The Challenge of Peace: God's Promise and Our Response is not only one of the most important pastoral letters ever to be issued by the National Conference of Catholic Bishops, it also represents a significant moment in the life and history of the American Catholic Church. In a sense, the American Catholic community "comes of age" with this Pastoral Letter. Addressing the sociopolitical arena, the Bishops do not hesitate to challenge certain key aspects of official United States policy regarding nuclear weapons; internally, the Pastoral Letter exhorts American Catholics to think critically and to come to some important decisions, in conscience, on questions of nuclear morality.

One indisputable sign of the American Catholic Church's "coming of age" is the process which the Bishops used to develop *Challenge of Peace*. A spirit of dialogue, reflection, consultation, and prayer marked the gradual but steady evolution of the Pastoral Letter. When the Bishops formally promulgated *Challenge of Peace* on May 3, 1983, they intended that that same spirit of dialogue would continue to permeate discussion of the Pastoral Letter and the complex question of modern warfare, as Cardinal Joseph Bernardin's Introduction to this book indicates. This volume of essays briskly takes the Bishops at their word. I purposely invited scholars whose positions vary on the question of the morality of nuclear warfare, deterrence, and disarmament in order to indicate to the reader the complexity of the issues and the wide spectrum of thought which currently exists among American Catholic theorists on nuclear-related topics. It will soon be obvious to the reader that certain theorists are more favorably disposed to *Challenge of Peace* than others. All theorists, however, take the American Catholic Bishops to be serious dialogical partners in the ongoing quest for moral clarity in a nuclear world.

Francis X. Winters, S. J. has traced the episcopal debate on nuclear morality for several years. In this book, he addresses the crucial question of deterrence. Winters presents the Second Vatican Council and Cardinal John Krol's 1979 testimony before the United States Senate Foreign Relations Committee hearing on SALT II as significant statements which set the direction for the American Catholic Bishops' 1983 stance. Winters then inspects the content of *Challenge of Peace* on the topic of deterrence and assesses the political impact which the Pastoral Letter might have on U.S. deterrent strategy.

William V. O'Brien has painstakingly investigated the question of morality and nuclear warfare since 1960. His chapter in this collection questions whether or not the Bishops have provided clear and helpful guidance to those who share the responsibility for the defense of the free world and that world's constituents.

Michael Novak argues that the nuclear policies of the Catholic Bishops do not actually differ very much from those of successive U.S. governments. He chides the Bishops, however, for paying scant attention to the quantity, quality, location, and activities of Soviet armed power.

Francis X. Meehan takes up the Letter's statement that just-war theory and pacifism are in "complementary relationship" to one another. He pushes beyond the Pastoral Letter to explore the possibility of a Catholic endorsement of nonviolence as a basic moral stance.

My chapter examines the Bishops' teaching on the morality of use and compares/contrasts that teaching with the positions of contemporary American Catholic theorists on the issue. I then assess the significance of the Letter and draw some implications from its teaching.

Several persons have been very supportive of my work in editing this collection of essays on the Pastoral Letter. I want to thank Cardinal Bernardin in a special way for his thoughtful introduction to the book. Francis X. Winters, S.J. encouraged the idea of this collection from the start and I am grateful for his support. John B. Breslin, S.J., Director of Georgetown University Press, graciously brought his expertise to this project and I have enjoyed working with him and with his fine staff. Finally, I want to express my gratitude to the American Catholic Bishops whose Pastoral Letter prompted this collection of essays, especially to the Ad Hoc Committee of Bishops who developed the Letter and to Reverend J. Bryan Hehir, staff person to the National Conference of Catholic Bishops, for the crucial role which he played in the evolution of *Challenge of Peace.*

A final word on the documentation of the Letter used in this text. I have employed a standardized form so that the reader can readily find the reference, regardless of which edition of the Pastoral Letter she/he is using (*Origins,* United States Catholic Conference, *National Catholic Reporter,* and so forth). The Roman numerals refer to the four main sections of the Letter. Documentation after the Roman numeral refers to subdivisions within that particular section of the Pastoral. The final number in all documentation refers to the numbered paragraphs in the United States Catholic Conference editions.

I hope that this collection of essays will be one contribution to the continuing dialogue regarding the morality of nuclear warfare, deterrence, and disarmament—dialogue vitally needed in a world desperately in search of peace.

Chestnut Hill College, Philadelphia   JUDITH A. DWYER
January, 1984.

Introduction

The American Bishops' Pastoral Letter, "The Challenge of Peace: God's Promise and Our Response," was conceived and brought to full term in a process of dialogue. It was not intended, however, that this open, broad, interdisciplinary exchange be terminated with the completion of the Pastoral. The Bishops consciously sought to foster dialogue within the Church and the broader society not only as part of the process for developing the document but also as the means of ensuring that the needed follow-up would take place.

There is now evidence that this latter goal is being realized. For example, during the 20-year period prior to 1980, when the decision was made to prepare the Pastoral, the amount of theological writing on the topic was minimal. Since then, however, the Bishops' debate has sparked widespread discussion in the theological community.

The reason the Bishops called for a continuation of the dialogue is quite simple. In the Pastoral we arrived at a number of specific conclusions on war and peace issues. While we believe these conclusions are consistent with the principles articulated in Catholic teaching, we readily admit that what we have said is not necessarily the last word. "The experience of preparing this letter," we stated, "has manifested to us the range of strongly held opinion in the Catholic community on questions of fact and judgment concerning issues of war and peace."

Not only do we want others to continue the dialogue; we ourselves intend to continue as participants in the theological exchange which is growing both in America and Europe. We also want to continue making our contribution to the public debate because, as we said in the Pastoral, "we are convinced that there is no satisfactory answer to the human problems of the nuclear age which fails to consider the moral and religious dimensions of the questions we face." This book, edited by Sister Judith Dwyer, underscores the fact that the dialogue intended by the Bishops, both inside and outside the Church, is going forward.

All the authors have participated in the ecclesial and public debate about nuclear war so I was somewhat familiar with their thinking even before they contributed to this book. I have found their essays, written subsequent to the publication of the Pastoral, informative and helpful. It is clear, of course, that the authors do not agree among themselves. And I can state, with equal clarity, that I do not agree with some of the conclusions they have drawn!

But that is precisely the reason why the debate must go forward and why I have welcomed the publication of this book as well as a number of other similar initiatives. While some of the views expressed are quite critical of the Pastoral, they all need to be aired as part of our effort to arrive at a clearer and more broadly based understanding of the complex and urgent issues confronting us today. Only in this way will there be a firm basis for maintaining and building the peace in the future.

JOSEPH CARDINAL BERNARDIN
Archbishop of Chicago

JUDITH A. DWYER, S.S.J.

"The Challenge of Peace" and the Morality of Using Nuclear Weapons

Judith A. Dwyer, S.S.J. holds a Ph.D. in theology from The Catholic University of America, where she completed her dissertation, "An Analysis of Nuclear Warfare in Light of the Traditional Just-War Theory: An American Roman Catholic Perspective." She is the author of several articles on the topic of nuclear warfare and has lectured at a number of universities on current issues in moral theology. Sister Dwyer currently teaches at Chestnut Hill College, Philadelphia.

Reflecting the compexity of the nuclear problem, our arguments in this pastoral must be detailed and nuanced; but our no to nuclear war must in the end be definitive and decisive.[1]

This statement from the recent American Catholic Bishops' Pastoral Letter, *The Challenge of Peace: God's Promise and Our Response,* aptly summarizes the Bishops' treatment of the moral dilemma of using nuclear weapons. Detailed and subtle analysis permeates the letter as the Bishops grapple with the question of whether or not it is ever moral to use any of the 50,000 nuclear weapons which currently exist in stockpiles scattered throughout the globe.[2] The Bishops admit the right and the duty of governments to practice self-defense against aggression, including defense by armed force if necessary, but the question remains: May a nation-state employ nuclear weapons as legitimate means of self-defense? Does the Bishops' "definitive and decisive no" translate into a proscription against all uses of nuclear weapons?

The Bishops, aware of the various strategies for fighting nuclear war, carefully delineate their position in light of traditional just-war principles, an attempt which marks a fresh approach in American episcopal statements on this crucial issue. Earlier pastoral letters—*Human Life in Our Day, To Live in Christ Jesus: A Pastoral Reflection on the Moral Life* and John Cardinal Krol's Congressional testimony in behalf of the United States Catholic Conference [USCC]—while important developments in Catholic analysis of modern warfare, neglected to situate their investigations explicitly within the framework of traditional just-war theory.[3]

Just-war teaching attempts to prevent war but recognizes that in certain very restricted circumstances, the presumption in favor of peace and against war must be overridden.[4] If war cannot rationally be avoided, the teaching seeks to restrict and reduce its horror by providing a set of rigorous conditions which must be met if the decision to go to war is to be morally permissible. Known as *jus ad bellum* criteria, these conditions require a just cause, declaration of war by competent authority, an analysis of comparative justice, right intention which seeks the restoration of peace, the exhaustion of all peaceful alternatives, the probability of success and an assessment of proportionality, that is, a decision that the good expected by taking up arms outweighs the damages to be inflicted and the costs incurred by war.

Just-war teaching also provides conditions which must be met during combat. These *jus in bello* criteria include the principles of discrimination and proportionality. Discrimination protects the immunity of noncombatants from direct military attack by restricting direct targeting to combatants, military installations and factories whose products are directly related to the war effort. The *jus in bello* principle of proportionality demands an assessment of the good and evil consequences which can reasonably be foreseen as resulting from specific actions in warfare.

In light of these *jus ad bellum* and *jus in bello* principles of traditional just-war theory, the Bishops analyze the morality of modern warfare. Counterpopulation warfare, whether nuclear or conventional, is unequivocally condemned as immoral. This condemnation reiterates Vatican II's teaching that "any act of war aimed indiscriminately at the destruction of entire cities or of extensive areas along with their population is a crime against God and man itself."[5] While the National Conference of Catholic Bishops [NCCB] echoed the Council in the Pastoral Letters *Human Life in Our Day* and *To Live in Christ Jesus,* as did Krol's testimony before Congress in 1979, *Challenge of Peace* more sharply cites counterpopulation warfare as a violation of the traditional principle of discrimination. Moreover, *Challenge of Peace* specifically names certain groups within the human community who retain the right of immunity from direct military attack. Insists the Pastoral Letter: "Not even by the broadest definition can one rationally consider combatant entire classes of human beings such as schoolchildren, hospital patients, the elderly, the ill, the average industrial worker producing goods not directly related to military purposes, farmers, and many others."[6] Underlying this teaching are the perspectives and principles which the Bishops clearly set out in the Pastoral's first section: human life is sacred; the innate dignity of human beings is to be reverenced; human rights, including the right of innocent human beings to life, are to be protected. Therefore, one ought not to use or intend to use nuclear weapons directly against innocent persons.[7] This proscription against any form of counterpopulation warfare includes retaliatory action; the United States may not directly strike enemy cities even after our own cities have been struck, since no end justifies the use of means which are evil in themselves. The Bishops, however, do not apply the principle of discrimination to actual nuclear strategies or to the use of particular nuclear weapons, since such an application would entail a contingent judgment.

By reaffirming the principle of noncombatant immunity, the Pastoral Letter clearly rejects any attempt to relativize discrimination as a principle of justice which ought to govern activity in modern warfare, a position embraced by Georgetown University professor of government William V. O'Brien, who holds that the literal application of the principle of discrimination is incompatible with nuclear war. Noncombatant immunity is not an ironclad principle, according to O'Brien, but rather one which "enjoins us to concentrate our attack on military objectives and to minimize our destruction of noncombatants and civilian targets."[8]

The Pastoral Letter is also clear in its condemnation of "first use" of nuclear weapons, a condemnation which moves beyond the teaching of Vatican II and any previous American episcopal statement. The Bishops "do not perceive any situation in which the deliberate initiation of nuclear warfare on however restricted a scale can be morally justified. Nonnuclear attacks by another state must be resisted by other than nuclear means."[9] The rationale for this position is the Bishops' oft-repeated "extreme skepticism" about the prospects of controlling nuclear exchange.[10] The risk of escalation, rooted in human sinfulness and made readily accessible by the technology of the weapons systems, is so great that it leads the Bishops to condemn initiating nuclear war. Implicit in this judgment is the assessment that the proximate danger of escalation outweighs any good which might be accomplished by first use of nuclear weapons. Initiation of nuclear warfare, therefore, is disproportionate.

The Bishops clearly distinguish the conclusion that a nation ought not to initiate nuclear war from principles which admit of no exception (discrimination, proportionality). The Pastoral admits that the "no first use" judgment is a prudential one, based on specific circumstances which can be interpreted by people of good will in different manners. On the morality of first use, the Bishops allow for different opinions while reaching their own conclusion, one based on study, reflection and consultation, that such action involves a disporportionate risk to the human family.

This distinction in the Pastoral between general principles which admit of no exception and conclusions which are prudential judgments based on an assessment of factual data, therefore admitting of legitimate options, is a direct response to criticism which earlier drafts of the letter received regarding a lack of clarity on this matter. That criticism, received at the Rome Consultation on Peace and Disarmament and offered in a spirit of collegiality, called on the American Bishops to state clearly the different levels of authority which exist within the Pastoral Letter and to do so in respect for the freedom of the Christian so that he/she could be clearly informed about what is binding in conscience. This distinction would also respect the integrity of the Catholic faith so that nothing would be proposed as doctrine of the Church that pertains to prudential judgments or alternative choices; similarly, the teaching authority which belongs to each bishop would not wrongly be applied, thereby obscuring its credibility.[11]

Having condemned counterpopulation warfare and the first use of nuclear weapons, *Challenge of Peace* examines a third possible use of nuclear weapons: retaliatory use in a limited counterforce exchange. In contrast to counterpopulation warfare, counterforce strategies target missiles directly against the enemy's combatant forces, military bases, and defense-related industries. The Bishops question the *real* possibility of a "limited nuclear exchange" against the *theoretical* possibility and raise a series of questions which challenge the actual meaning of "limited."[12] Once again, the Bishops make a prudential judgment on the morality of "limited nuclear warfare" as they implicitly apply the principle of proportionality to the concrete situation. They recognize that the policy debate on the question of the practical feasibility of waging limited nuclear war is "inconclusive" and that "all participants are left with hypothetical projections about the probable reactions in nuclear exchange." Nonetheless, the Bishops reiterate their great skepticism that a limited nuclear exchange would remain limited for very long; they question whether such an exchange could hold a "reasonable hope of success" for bringing about justice and peace; they argue that "the burden of proof remains on those who assert that meaningful limitation is possible."[13] The Bishops conclude their examination of "limited nuclear warfare" by noting the psychological and political significance of moving from conventional war into the nuclear arena in which the human community has no experience of control.[14] Asserting that the first imperative is to prevent any use of nuclear weapons, they express hope that leaders will resist the notion that nuclear conflict can be limited or won in any traditional sense.

Explicitly citing the principle of proportionality, the Bishops reject any type of counterforce exchange which would take place in heavily populated areas in which massive civilian casualties would occur. Such a strike, while not intentionally indiscriminate, violates the just-war principle of proportionality. The Bishops note that "While any judgment of proportionality is always open to differing evaluations, there are actions which can be decisively judged to be disproportionate."[15]

What the Bishops have *not* said is that *every possible use* of nuclear weapons is intrinsically evil (*malum in se*). While expressing "profound skepticism" about the moral acceptability of *any* use of nuclear weapons, the Bishops nevertheless refrain from stating that any use of nuclear weapons is immoral and therefore they do not embrace what moral philosopher John Langan has termed the "absolutist" position.[16] In fact, a proposal by Archbishop John Quinn that argued for less ambiguity and for a straightforward condemnation of any use of nuclear weapons was defeated during the special episcopal meeting which voted on the final version of *Challenge of Peace*.[17]

Why do the Bishops refrain from a clear condemnation of any use of nuclear weapons, a position which undoubtedly disappoints the pacifist community?[18] While the overall thrust of the document is against any use, the Bishops deem it necessary for the sake of deterrence to remain ambiguous on this point. In response to the Quinn proposal that the Pastoral Letter express "opposition on moral grounds to any use of nuclear weapons," Cardinal Joseph L. Bernardin, Chair of the *ad hoc* Committee of Bishops charged with the development of the Pastoral Letter (hereafter cited as the Bernardin Committee) insisted that "the note of ambiguity must remain," given "the paradox of the nuclear issue."[19] Should the Bishops unequivocally condemn any use of nuclear weapons, then deterrence becomes ineffective, an empty bluff since the deterrent is credible only insofar as the enemy believes that some nuclear weapons will be used, should the deterrent fail. *Challenge of Peace* neither condemns the deterrent nor calls for unilateral disarmament. Logically then, the Bishops must leave open the question of any use of nuclear weapons. They do not explicitly oppose every use of nuclear weapons; neither do they list any cases in which "use" would be considered moral.[20] Capturing the paradox of the nuclear issue, that nuclear weapons are maintained in order to prevent use, the Bishops deliberately leave a note of ambiguity regarding the moral licitness of any use of nuclear weapons, a subtlety missed by the *New York Times'* editorial "Bishops and the Bomb," which criticized the naiveté of the Bishops' condemnation of any use of nuclear weapons.[21]

American Catholic Theorists on the Morality of Using Nuclear Weapons

How does the position embraced in *Challenge of Peace* compare with positions held by leading American Roman Catholic theorists on the question of use?

Richard A. McCormick's "Notes on Moral Theology" concludes that "there is a growing conviction (popular, strategic, moral-theological) that any use of nuclear weapons is morally irresponsibile," a position with which McCormick concurs.[22] In addition to McCormick, other leading American Catholic theorists—J. Bryan Hehir, Francis X. Winters, David Hollenbach, and Charles Curran—embrace this conviction and do so by analyzing nuclear warfare in light of traditional just-war principles.

J. Bryan Hehir, Associate Secretary for the Office of International Peace and Justice, USCC, and staff person to the NCCB, preserves the traditional just-war principles of discrimination and proportionality but "supports them" by citing the psychological consequences of crossing the firebreak between conventional and nuclear weapons.[23] The very introduction of nuclear weapons into combat means a *qualitative* change in the nature of warfare itself. The moral imperative of this era, therefore, is to prevent any use of nuclear weapons; Hehir condemns any new technological development which might make nuclear war more "thinkable" (neutron bomb, cruise missile) since to stress "limited damage" is to reduce the psychological/political barrier between conventional and nuclear weapons.[24] In order to avoid the need to resort to "the nuclear option," Hehir supports a build-up of conventional weapons, especially in such troubled areas as the Mideast. Should deterrence fail, however, Hehir believes that the United States should surrender rather than use immoral means, that is, nuclear weapons.

Although he once argued for the justifiable use of nuclear weapons in counterstrategic defense,[25] Francis X. Winters now condemns all uses of nuclear weapons on the basis of principles of discrimination and proportionality.[26] Winters is especially perceptive in his analysis of the relative paucity and probable invulnerability of "combatants" in a nuclear exchange.[27]

It is proportionality, however, which remains the "fundamental criterion" for evaluating the morality of using "small" nuclear weapons, according to Winters. Citing government documents and the predicted physical effects of using nuclear weapons, the theorist concludes that there is no predictable way to assess the damages of even a "limited" nuclear exchange; assessment of proportionality remains impossible. Like Hehir, Winters encourages a strong build-up of conventional power and suggests that a deterrent strategy might include conventional warheads mounted on MaRVed strategic weapons targeted at Soviet industrial/transportation/military centers.

Winters limits his analysis to counterforce nuclear warfare and does not consider the isolated use of a small, tactical nuclear weapon against a military target. It would be helpful to the overall analysis of the problem if Winters were to inspect this specific use of a nuclear weapon, either by assessing it against the principle of proportionality or by considering Hehir's argument for "psychological criteria" as support for proportionality and discrimination.

David Hollenbach's contributions to the debate have been to indicate the complementary nature of just-war theory and pacifism, to study the question of use from different methodological perspectives, and to analyze carefully the use of nuclear weapons in light of *jus ad bellum* and *jus in bello* principles.[28] Hollenbach condemns counterpopulation warfare on the basis of discrimination, reinforced by proportionality, and argues that even the limited use of strategic nuclear weapons violates the *jus ad bellum* principle of "reasonable hope of success" as well as the *jus in bello* principle of proportionality, since the risk of escalation is ever-present. This likelihood of escalation also proscribes first use of nuclear weapons in the European theater. In dialogue with John Langan, Hollenbach admits that one might hypothesize a case in which use of nuclear weapons would not violate just-war principles; he contends, nevertheless, that such a hypothesis has little or nothing to do with the *real* international situation.[29] Hollenbach rejects the argument that "moral responsibility" for the harm which war causes lies solely with the aggressor since limits remain on what can be done even in defense of just cause; these limits are both moral and political. He maintains a "no use" stance in light of the strong evidence from strategic studies regarding the consequences of any use of a nuclear weapon, although he admits his position includes prudential judgments which cannot be subject to logically certain demonstration. Concludes Hollenbach: "The escalatory dangers which attend any use of nuclear weapons make their employment irrational from a political view as well as unacceptable from the perspective of basic moral values and *prima facie* duties."[30]

Charles E. Curran first takes up the issue in dialogue with Paul Ramsey.[31] Curran finds himself "more hesitant" than Ramsey to admit the morality of using multimegaton nuclear weapons; he criticizes the Princeton scholar for failing to seek to limit collateral civilian casualties as much as possible, for neglecting the danger of escalation, and for questioning the competence of both the Church and the ethicist to address political issues. In a subsequent essay,[32] Curran proscribes the use of large nuclear weapons on the basis of discrimination and proportionality; he does not, however, address the use of smaller nuclear weapons but implies that he supports the licity of their use. Recent contributions by Curran now clearly condemn the use of *all* nuclear weapons in light of traditional just-war principles.[33]

Catholic theorists William V. O'Brien and John Langan reject the position which proscribes all use of nuclear weapons. Their thesis agrees with earlier Catholic theorists who examined the issue and who concluded, in a variety of ways, that certain uses of nuclear weapons would not violate just-war principles of discrimination or proportionality.[34]

Georgetown University professor William V. O'Brien has painstakingly investigated the morality of nuclear weapons since 1960.[35] O'Brien holds discrimination to be a "relative prescription"; the principle of proportionality remains more crucial for testing the justifiability of certain uses of nuclear weapons. Under this principle, O'Brien can envision the discrete use of tactical, theater, or even strategic, counterforce nuclear weapons, warning that such an assessment must always be made in the full context of contemplated use and probable effects of such use.[36] While such a position appears to give wide latitude to use, it nevertheless represents a shift in O'Brien's stance—a stance which once justified retaliatory, strategic, *countervalue* attacks.[37] O'Brien continues to maintain that a finding that nuclear warfare is intrinsically evil would be valid only if it could be shown that such warfare "inevitably escapes control"; such proof, however, is impossible. Concluding that a strong moral presumption exists against use, O'Brien insists that nuclear warfare cannot be deemed to be *malum in se*.[38]

The writings of John Langan of Woodstock Theological Center are sensitive to the complexity of the question.[39] In contrast to what he calls the "absolutist" position, Langan embraces the "contextualist" approach. Central to this stance is his opinion that "it is comparatively easy to construct hypothetical cases in which nuclear weapons are used against specifically military targets" in a way that does not violate tradtional just-war principles.[40] Although Langan can imagine some hypothetical cases which would permit use, he nevertheless condemns three actions: (1) the destruction of the human race in a catastrophic, nuclear exchange or the definitive pollution of the human environment; (2) the destruction of entire societies; (3) attacks inflicted against noncombatants or which produce environmental consequences that ultimately may destroy large numbers of human lives.[41]

Two weaknesses plague Langan's theory. The first remains the *real* versus the theoretical possibility of fighting a discriminate and proportionate nuclear war.[42] The second weakness is Langan's assessment of the "absolutist" position. The condemnation of all use does not necessarily lead to the conclusion that possession, production, and deployment of all nuclear weapons are wrong or that Catholics must refrain from cooperating in weapons' production. Similarly, a proscription against use does not necessarily lead to a call for unilateral disarmament.[43]

When tested against the theorists' positions, *Challenge of Peace* emerges as a document in the "spirit" of Hehir, Winters, Hollenbach, and Curran. Although the letter refrains from an outright condemnation of all use, it certainly echoes aspects of these theorists' arguments. *Challenge of Peace* discusses the psychological consequences of crossing into an arena of warfare in which there exists no human experience; it opposes weapons systems which blur the difference between nuclear and conventional weapons (Hehir). Limited nuclear warfare violates the *jus ad bellum* criterion of "reasonable hope of success"; its risk of escalation remains disproportionate (Hollenbach). The letter documents its position by citing key statements from the United States government and military sectors, resources which Winters has consistently used in his own analysis of the problem. Finally, the Bishops clearly see it as within their proper role to address a problem which has obvious military and political aspects but which also involves fundamental moral choices (Curran).

Significance of the Pastoral Letter

It would be unrealistic to see the Bishops' teaching in *Challenge of Peace* as the final word on the subject of nuclear warfare.[44] The Bishops themselves do not see the Pastoral in that light; it is, for them, only the serious dialogue which must surround this crucial issue.[45] They envision *Challenge of Peace* as a contribution to an emerging "theology of peace," enfleshing Vatican II's call to evaluate war with an entirely new attitude, a call to which *Human Life in Our Day* and *To Live in Christ Jesus* were responses.

As a "first step" toward confronting an exceptionally serious moral problem, however, *Challenge of Peace* is significant in three ways. For the first time in the development of a pastoral letter, the American Catholic Bishops employed a process of dialogue, shared reflection, and consultation which involved any Catholic who wished to participate. All Catholics were free to write to their local bishops or to a member of the Bernardin Committee to express a viewpoint on any one of the three drafts which preceded the final version of the letter. Criticism of the drafts was actively solicited in certain dioceses. In addition to inviting participation from the Catholic community, the Bernardin Committee also heard testimony from a variety of witnesses in the political and military sectors. Bryan Hehir, Director of the International Peace and Justice Office, USCC, summarizes the thinking of several commentators: "the process of the debate generated in the Church, and by extension in American society, will have greater long-term significance than the final version of the letter itself."[46]

If the Pastoral's process of development reflects a more participative model of Church, the letter itself represents a shift from documents paternalistic in tone to a pronouncement whose teaching addresses the mature Catholic conscience, a second significant feature of *Challenge of Peace*. This refreshing shift is especially evident in the entire fourth section of the letter, "The Pastoral Challenge and Response," and in those segments of the letter in which the Bishops distinguish certain conclusions (no first use) from principles which admit of no exception (discrimination, proportionality).

A third point of significance centers on the Pastoral's direct challenge not only to specific policies of the United States government but also to the values and principles that structure a growing nuclear militarism.[47] In condemning first use of nuclear weapons, the Bishops stress the qualitative difference between conventional and nuclear war and react against the view that nuclear war is "likely" and "more acceptable."[48] They also directly challenge current NATO strategy in the European theater, a conflict acknowledged by the episcopacy. *Challenge of Peace* nevertheless urges NATO to move rapidly toward adoption of a "no first use" policy, although it recognizes that this policy will take time to implement and will require the development of an adequate alternative defense posture.[49]

This call in the Pastoral Letter to develop "an adequate alternative defense posture," however, moves beyond some strategists' advocacy of a conventional force buildup. Acknowledging that a strengthening of conventional defenses may be a proportionate price to pay if this were to reduce the possibility of a nuclear war, the letter refrains from drawing a conclusion on what it terms a "technical debate."[50] From the perspective of a developing theology of peace, the Bishops express instead the belief that "any program directed at reducing reliances on nuclear weapons is not likely to succeed unless it includes measures to reduce tensions and to work for the balanced reduction of conventional forces."[51]

Implications of the Pastoral Letter

What are the implications of *Challenge of Peace*'s teaching regarding the use of nuclear weapons for Catholics who serve in the armed forces or who work in defense-related industries? Noting that defense policy exists to defend the peace and that military personnel should understand their vocation this way, the Pastoral nevertheless reminds all in authority and in the chain of command that military manuals prohibit certain actions in warfare, especially actions which inflict harm on innocent persons.[52] Moreover, *Challenge of Peace* teaches that refusal to take unlawful or forbidden measures in warfare should be viewed as courageous, patriotic action, not as cowardly or treasonous behavior. Invoking just-war principles, the Bishops exhort military personnel to exhaust every peaceful alternative before war is even remotely considered; battle strategies ought to be both discriminating and proportionate. The Pastoral Letter also advocates appropriate training and education of combat forces, outrightly rejecting any attempt to dehumanize the nation's military personnel with training which dulls sensibilities and generates hatred toward adversaries. The Bishops conclude their address to military personnel by expressing their gratitude for the sacrifices which so many in military service must make today.[53]

Questions also arise for Catholics employed by industries which develop or produce weapons of mass destruction. Neither presuming nor pretending that clear answers exist for the many personal, professional, and financial choices confronting such employees, the letter reiterates its condemnation of certain uses of nuclear weapons while also expressing a conditioned moral acceptance of deterrence. In light of such teaching, "All Catholics, at every level of defense industries, can and should use the moral principles of this letter to form their consciences."[54] The Bishops here recognize the possibility of pluralism since different people are faced with different judgments and will arrive at diverse decisions on so complex a matter. The Bishops promise support to those who decide to resign from employment as well as to employees who remain in defense-related industries.

The implications of *Challenge of Peace* for the broader Catholic community are exceedingly rich and revolve around three significant areas: educational, ecumenical, and political.

Crucial to the overall impact of the Pastoral are the balanced, objective educational programs on the content of *Challenge of Peace* which the Bishops have mandated for Catholics of every age. The community must study the Pastoral in all its complexity. Primary responsibility for this matter rests with the individual Bishops who are to see that the Pastoral becomes a "living document" at the local level. The educational process will vary with each diocese but the fact that such education should take place is nonnegotiable.

The same openness, concern and complexity which characterize the Pastoral Letter should be evident in any educational program on its content. Not only is it important that Catholics know *what* the Bishops have said; it is equally imperative that Catholics understand *why* the Bishops reached certain conclusions in the Pastoral. The principle of discrimination and its respect for innocent human life must be clearly understood by Catholics and seen as part of the overall "respect for life" teaching which characterizes Catholic tradition. The principle of proportionality, the obligation to assess and weigh carefully the good and evil consequences of specific actions, must be presented with all of its ramifications: the need for study, prayer, reflection, consultation.

Challenge of Peace should serve as a catalyst for the revitalization of the American Catholic Church. It calls upon Catholics to engage in serious reflection on matters of the utmost concern and to come to some very important decisions, in conscience, about issues related to modern warfare. Similarly, if the developing "theology of peace" about which the Pastoral frequently speaks is to emerge beyond the seminal stage, it is imperative that Catholics take up the proposals and policies advanced in the third section of the letter.[55] Catholics should envision the Pastoral as a challenge to their hands and hearts and minds to fashion a better world in which the principles and proposals presented in the letter move from print into practice.

Promulgation of the Pastoral Letter opens wide the possibility of fertile ecumenical dialogue on this issue. The initial response to *Challenge of Peace* from the Protestant community has been generally favorable. *Christianity and Crisis* editorialized that the document "has a claim on the attention of others besides Catholics," while James M. Wall praised the Bishops' involvement in "the primary problem of our time."[56] John C. Bennett expressed the belief that *Challenge of Peace* could persuade people outside the Catholic constituency because the Bishops "did not issue an ecclesiastical edict" but came to their position "by a process that non-Catholics, both religious and secular, can appreciate . . . three drafts, open discussion, listening to people from all sides, and final debate among themselves that the public could hear."[57] The Episcopalian, Lutheran, United Methodist, American Baptist, and United Presbyterian Churches have recently issued statements on the moral dimensions of nuclear war, the arms race, deterrence.[58] In addition to these Christian denominations which have always recognized the possibility of some legitimate use of force in self-defense, the traditional "peace churches," for example, the Quaker and Mennonite Churches, have made significant contributions to the debate. This moment of increased interfaith dialogue and witness on so crucial an issue should not be missed by the American Catholic community.[59]

Finally, the Pastoral is clear in its call to American Catholics to remain politically astute, evaluating national goals and policies in light of the deepest values cherished by the Catholic community: peace, justice, and security for the entire human family. Recognizing the legitimacy of their own involvement in this moral question which is also embedded in public policy, the Bishops encourage the wider Catholic community to stay vitally alive as patriotic citizens of both the United States and the world.[60]

The implications for the wider political community are more difficult to discern at present. Writing recently in *Foreign Affairs,* L. Bruce van Voort predicted that, given the involvement of so many churches in the nuclear question, "no government in Washington can afford not to pay attention; no statesman can be indifferent to the debate." Van Voort continues:

> In this context, then, the current course of the Catholic Church and many Protestant denominations, if continued, may result in the most direct intervention in strategic and foreign policies in this nation's history. One can suggest more: because of their enormous memberships, organization, and dedication, the role of the Churches will become crucial in determining the political impact and outcome of the "nuclear movement" in the United States.[61]

Whether van Voort's prediction comes true remains to be seen; it is safe to say, however, that *Challenge of Peace* has already caused some concern for the Reagan administration.[62] This concern, coupled with the widespread media attention given to the Letter and its development, indicates that the Catholic Bishops have struck a sensitive political chord. A truer test of the impact of *Challenge of Peace* will be whether or not public officials take up the specific initiative suggested in the Pastoral, that is, the establishment of a task force to consider the problems and challenges posed by nuclear disarmament to the country's economic well-being and industrial output. Further, will the United States government heed the Pastoral's request that this country propose to the United Nations the establishment of an international taskforce for peace?

Challenge of Peace remains a subtle and sophisticated piece of teaching and in that, does justice to the complexity of the topic which it addresses. The American Catholic community can be grateful for this bold but balanced Pastoral which neither evades historical responsibility nor compromises the tradition of the Church. *Challenge of Peace* and its teaching regarding the morality of using nuclear weapons remains just that, a challenge. The Catholic community and the human community as a whole can do no better than to respond with as much sensitivity and concern as have been evidenced by the Bishops in this Pastoral Letter.

NOTES

1. National Conference of Catholic Bishops, *The Challenge of Peace: God's Promise and Our Response* (Washington, D.C.: United States Catholic Conference, 1983), II, A, 138.

2. Ruth Leger Sivard, *World Military and Social Expenditures, 1982* (Leesburg, Va.: World Priorities, 1982), pp. 10–13. See also The International Institute for Strategic Studies, *The Military Balance 1982–1983* (London: The International Institute for Strategic Studies, 1982).

3. National Conference of Catholic Bishops, *Human Life in Our Day* (Washington, D.C.: United States Catholic Conference, 1968); *To Live in Christ Jesus: A Pastoral Reflection on the Moral Life* (Washington, D.C.: United States Catholic Conference, 1976); John Cardinal Krol, "SALT II: Statement of Support," *Origins* 9 (September 6, 1979), pp. 195–99. Other American episcopal statements on the question of modern warfare are "A Statement on Peace," *Catholic Mind* 65 (February 1967), pp. 62–63; United States Catholic Conference Administrative Board, "The Gospel of Peace and the Danger of War," *Origins* 7 (March 2, 1978), pp. 579–80. See also "The Bishops on Peace," *America* 115 (December 3, 1966), p. 728. For a helpful summary of Church statements, see Robert Heyer, ed. *Nuclear Disarmament: Key Statements of Popes, Bishops, Councils, and Churches* (Ramsey, N.J.: Paulist Press, 1982).

4. For historical background on just-war tradition, see the excellent studies by James T. Johnson, *Ideology, Reason and the Limitation of War* (Princeton: Princeton University Press, 1975) and *Just War Tradition and the Limitation of War* (Princeton: Princeton University Press, 1981). See also J. Bryan Hehir's thoughtful study, "The Just-War Ethic and Catholic Theology: Dynamics of Change and Continuity," in *War or Peace? The Search for New Answers*, ed. Thomas A. Shannon (Maryknoll, N.Y.: Orbis, 1980), pp. 15–39.

5. "The Pastoral Constitution on the Church in the Modern World," in *The Gospel of Peace and Justice: Catholic Social Teaching since Pope John*, ed. Joseph Gremillion (Maryknoll, N.Y.: Orbis, 1976), pp. 316–17.

6. NCCB, *Challenge of Peace*, I, C3, 108. For a similar argument issued during World War II, see John C. Ford, "The Morality of Obliteration Bombing," *Theological Studies* 5 (September 1944), pp. 261–309.

7. This condemnation of "intention to use" is crucial when the Pastoral Letter addresses the issue of deterrence. See *Challenge of Peace*, II, D, 162–99.

8. William V. O'Brien, "Just-War Doctrine in a Nuclear Context," *Theological Studies* 44 (June 1983), pp. 211–12. See also O'Brien's *The Conduct of Just and Limited War* (New York: Praeger, 1981), pp. 45–47.

9. NCCB, *Challenge of Peace*, II, B2, 150.

10. In note 61 which accompanies the text of *Challenge of Peace*, the Bishops provide documentation to support their "extreme skepticism" about the feasibility of limiting nuclear war. Defense documents have admitted the possibility that nuclear war could become "uncontrollable." The first such public admission of this fact is found in U.S. Arms Control and Disarmament Agency, *Worldwide Effects of Nuclear War . . . Some Perspectives* (Washington, D.C.: U.S. Government Printing

Office, 1974). This document notes the possibility of blackout of high-frequency radio communication through disruption of the ionosphere by nuclear blasts.

   11. See "January Meeting in Rome on the War and Peace Pastoral," *Origins* 12 (April 7, 1983), pp. 690–91. This meeting included participants from the United States (Archbishop John Roach, Joseph Cardinal Bernardin, Monsignor Daniel Hoye, Reverend Brian Hehir) as well as representatives from European bishops' conferences (France, Great Britain, West Germany, Belgium, Italy, and The Netherlands) and Vatican officials. The meeting was held in Rome on January 18–19, 1983. See "A Vatican Synthesis," *Origins* 12 (April 7, 1983), pp. 691–95. For an excellent comparative study of the positions of various episcopal conferences, see Francis X. Winters, S.J., "Nuclear Deterrence Morality: Atlantic Community Bishops in Tension," *Theological Studies* 43 (September 1982), pp. 428–46.

   12. NCCB, *Challenge of Peace*, II, B3, 157–58.

   13. For similar argumentation, see David Hollenbach, S.J., *Nuclear Ethics: A Christian Moral Argument* (Ramsey, N.J.: Paulist Press, 1983), pp. 47–62. Hollenbach's other contributions to serious moral analysis of the question of nuclear warfare include "Nuclear Weapons and Nuclear War: The Shape of the Catholic Debate," *Theological Studies* 43 (December 1982), pp. 577–605 and "Nuclear Weapons: Policy and Christian Conscience," *New Catholic World* 226 (January/February 1983), pp. 17–20.

   14. J. Bryan Hehir has long argued that "psychological criteria" ought to be considered when evaluating the morality of using nuclear weapons. See Robert A. Gessert and J. Bryan Hehir, *The New Nuclear Debate* (New York: Council of Religion and International Affairs, 1976), pp. 47–53.

   15. NCCB, *Challenge of Peace,* II, D, 181–82.

   16. John Langan, S.J., "The American Hierarchy and Nuclear Weapons," *Theological Studies* 43 (September 1982), pp. 447–67.

   17. Patty Edmonds, "Bishops Commit Church to Peace," *National Catholic Reporter* (13 May 1983), p. 19.

   18. "Pacifist" here refers both to the "absolute pacifist," that is, one who holds that all war, nuclear and conventional, is immoral and to the "nuclear pacifist," that is, one who maintains that the use of some force against aggression is justifiable but that the use of nuclear weapons surpasses reasonable measures of defense.

   19. Patty Edmonds, "Bishops Commit Church to Peace," p. 19.

   20. Thomas J. Reese, "The Bishops' 'Challenge of Peace'," *America* 148 (May 21, 1983), p. 394.

   21. "Bishops and the Bomb," *The New York Times* (May 6, 1983), sec. A, p. 30. Noted the *Times*, "They [the Bishops] accept possession of nuclear weapons to deter a Soviet nuclear attack, pending complete disarmament. But they also characterize any use of nuclear weapons as immoral, thus emboldening Archbishop John Quinn to call upon Catholics in the armed forces to reject any order to fire them. The obvious contradiction is that a weapon than can in no circumstances be fired cannot very well deter an attack."

   22. Richard A. McCormick, "Notes on Moral Theology, 1982," *Theological Studies* 44 (March 1983), p. 110.

23. Robert A. Gessert and J. Bryan Hehir, *The New Nuclear Debate*, pp. 49–50.

24. J. Bryan Hehir, "The Catholic Church and the Arms Race," *Worldview* 21 (July-August 1978), pp. 13–18; "P.D. 59: New Issue in an Old Argument," *Worldview* 23 (November 1980), pp. 10–12.

25. Francis X. Winters, "Morality in the War Room," *America* 132 (February 15, 1975), pp. 106–10.

26. Francis X. Winters, "The Nuclear Arms Race: Man Versus War Machines," *Worldview* 19 (September 1976), pp. 22–26.

27. "Morality in the War Room," p. 109.

28. David Hollenbach, "Nuclear Weapons and Nuclear War: The Shape of the Catholic Debate," pp. 577–605; "Nuclear Weapons: Policy and Christian Conscience," pp. 17–20; *Nuclear Ethics: A Christian Moral Argument.*

29. *Nuclear Ethics: A Christian Moral Argument*, pp. 47–49.

30. *Ibid.*, p. 60.

31. Charles E. Curran, *Politics, Medicine, and Christian Ethics: A Dialogue with Paul Ramsey* (Philadelphia: Fortress Press, 1973).

32. Charles E. Curran, "The Fifth Commandment: Thou Shall Not Kill," in *Ongoing Revision in Moral Theology* (Notre Dame: Fides Press, 1975), pp. 168–72.

33. Charles E. Curran, "A Complex Document for a 'Big Church'," *Commonweal* 109 (August 13, 1982), pp. 438–39; *American Catholic Social Ethics: Twentieth Century Approaches* (Notre Dame, Ind.: University of Notre Dame Press, 1982).

34. See, for instance, Francis J. Connell, "Is the H-Bomb Right or Wrong?" *Sign* 29 (March 1950), pp. 11–13; "Problems of War," *American Ecclesiastical Review* 125 (July 1951), pp. 64–65; "Weapons of Destruction," *Today* 9 (November 1958), pp. 246–51; John R. Connery, "Morality of Nuclear Armament," *Theology Digest* 5 (Winter 1957), pp. 9–12; John C. Ford, "The Hydrogen Bombing of Cities," *Theology Digest* 5 (Winter 1957), pp. 6–9; Gerald Kelly, "Notes on Moral Theology," *Theological Studies* 10 (March 1949), pp. 77–80; John Courtney Murray, "Remarks on the Moral Problem of War," *Theological Studies* 20 (1959), pp. 40–60; Thomas E. Murray, "Morality and Security: A Forgotten Equation," *America* 96 (December 1, 1956), pp. 258–62; "Rational Nuclear Armament," *Catholic Mind* 55 (September-October, 1957), pp. 387–97.

35. William V. O'Brien, "Force, Yes, Violence, No," *Social Order* 10 (November 1960), pp. 415–18; "The Role of Force in International Juridical Order," *Catholic Lawyer* 6 (Winter 1960), pp. 22–32; "The Nuclear Dilemma: Nuclear War and the Conflict of Conscience," *Social Order* 13 (February 1963), pp. 45–8; "The Fate of Counterforce," *Commonweal* 78 (May 17, 1963), pp. 216–18; "Instrument of International Politics," *Worldview* 6 (May 1963), pp. 2–6; *Nuclear War, Deterrence, and Morality* (Westminster, Md.: Newman Press, 1967); *War and/or Survival* (New York: Doubleday, 1969).

36. William V. O'Brien, "Just-War Doctrine in a Nuclear Context," pp. 191–220.

37. William V. O'Brien, *The Conduct of Just and Limited War*, p. 135.

38. "Just-War Doctrine in a Nuclear Context," p. 212–13.

39. John Langan, "A Useful Benchmark of Catholic Thinking," *Commonweal*

109 (August 13, 1982), pp. 424–26; "The Debate Indentified," *Washington Quarterly* 5 (Autumn 1982), pp. 123–27; "The American Hierarchy and Nuclear Weapons," pp. 447–67.

40. "The American Hierarchy and Nuclear Weapons," pp. 454–55.

41. *Ibid.*, pp. 461–62.

42. This criticism is made by both Richard A. McCormick in his "Notes on Moral Theology, 1982," and David Hollenbach, *Nuclear Ethics: A Christian Moral Argument*, p. 48.

43. See, for instance, the theory of J. Bryan Hehir.

44. Charles E. Curran makes this point in his "The Bishops and the Bomb: A Complex Document for a 'Big Church'," pp. 438–40. Richard A. McCormick, S.J. expresses wholehearted agreement with Curran on this point in his "Notes on Moral Theology: 1982," pp. 100, 109.

45. NCCB, *Challenge of Peace*, p. 2. "This letter is a contribution to a wider common effort meant to call Catholics and all members of our political community to dialogue and specific decisions about this awesome question."

46. J. Bryan Hehir, "The Process and the Product," *Commonweal* 109 (December 17, 1982), p. 680.

47. Richard B. Miller, "Catholic Bishops on War," *The Bulletin of the Atomic Scientists* 39 (May 1983), p. 9.

48. This point was noted by the participants from the United States at the Rome Consultation on Peace and Disarmament. See "A Vatican Synthesis," pp. 691–95.

49. Such realism regarding the fact that a "no first use" policy by NATO would take time to develop was strongly encouraged at the Rome Consultation on Peace and Disarmament. See "A Positive and Helpful Exchange of Views," *Origins* 12 (April 7, 1983), p. 696. This article is a memorandum on the Consultation. The call for "no first use" policy by NATO has also come from former members of the defense/political community. See McGeorge Bundy, George F. Kennan, Robert S. McNamara, Gerard Smith, "Nuclear Weapons and the Atlantic Alliance," *Foreign Affairs* 60 (Summer 1982), pp. 1157–70.

50. For a sampling of the "technicalities," see the recent attempt by the editors of *The Economist* to work out a projection of what NATO would need "so that it could hold the line without the implied threat to fire those battlefield nuclear weapons." The projection centers on the need for extra military personnel and equipment. See "Without the Bomb," *The Economist* 284 (July 31, 1982), pp. 11–12; "Do You Sincerely Want to Be Non-Nuclear?" *The Economist* 284 (July 31, 1983), pp. 30–32.

51. NCCB, *Challenge of Peace*, III, A3, 218.

52. *Ibid.*, IV, C, 311.

53. For discussion of the ramifications of Church teaching for military personnel, see Francis X. Winters, S.J., "The Bow or the Cloud? American Bishops Challenge the Arms Race," *America* 145 (July 25, 1981), pp. 26–30.

54. NCCB, *Challenge of Peace*, IV, C, 318.

55. For this reason, *America* sees the third section of the Pastoral as "crucial"

to whether or not American Catholics come to embrace a "bolder and more morally enlightened approach to the nuclear challenge." "A Moment for Peacemaking," p. 390. For a different assessment of the third section, see Michael Novak, "The Bishops Speak Out," *National Review* 35 (June 10, 1983), p. 681.

56. "About This Issue," *Christianity and Crisis* 43 (May 2, 1983), p. 155. James M. Wall, "Catholic Bishops Revise Position," *The Christian Century* 100 (April 27, 1983), p. 392.

57. John C. Bennett, "The Bishops' Pastoral: A Response," *Christianity and Crisis* 43 (May 30, 1983), p. 203.

58. House of Bishops [Episcopal] Pastoral Letter, "Identity, Pilgrimage, and Peace," General Convention, 1982; Lutheran Church in America, "Resolution on War and Peace in a Nuclear Age," Fall 1982; Lutheran Church in America, Collateral Paper, "Peace, Power and Might: The Church and Global Politics in a Thermonuclear World," Fall 1982; Council of Bishops of the United Methodist Church, "Pastoral Letter to a People Called United Methodist," 1982; General Board of the American Baptist Churches, "American Baptist Resolution in Support of International Efforts for Peace and Disarmament," June 1982; United Presbyterian Church in the United States of America, "Extending Peacemaking through the 1980s," *Church and Society* 72 (July/August 1982), pp. 6–7; United Presbyterian Church, "Confronting Idolatry," *Church and Society* 72 (July/August 1982), pp. 10–12; United Presbyterian Church, "Peacemaking: The Believer's Calling," *Church and Society* 70 (July/August 1980), pp. 7–14.

59. For development of this point, see my "The Role of the American Churches in the Nuclear Weapons' Debate," in *The Nuclear Freeze Debate: Arms Control Issues for the 1980s*, ed. Paul M. Cole and William J. Taylor, Jr. (Boulder, Colo.: Westview Press, 1983), pp. 77–92.

60. NCCB, *Challenge of Peace*, IV, B1, 281–282; C, 326.

61. L. Bruce van Voort, "The Churches and Nuclear Deterrence," *Foreign Affairs* 61 (Spring 1983), p. 830.

62. Richard Halloran, "U.S. Tells Bishops Morality Is Guide on Nuclear Policy," *The New York Times* (November 17, 1982), sec. A, p. 1; sec. B, p. 4. This article reports the letter which William P. Clark, President Reagan's National Security Adviser, sent to the Catholic Bishops. The letter attempted to convince the Catholic Bishops that their Pastoral (second draft) reflected "fundamental misreadings of American policies," and indeed that "moral considerations" did in fact shape government policies.

FRANCIS X. WINTERS, S.J.

The American Bishops on Deterrence—"Wise as Serpents, Innocent as Doves"

Francis X. Winters, S.J., is Associate Professor of Moral Theology and of International Relations, the School of Foreign Service, Georgetown University. He served as a consultant to the Bernardin Committee and has lectured on ethics and nuclear strategy at the Army, Navy and National War Colleges, the Department of State, the CIA and the RAND Corporation. He is the co-editor (with Harold P. Ford) and a contributor to *Ethics and Nuclear Strategy?* (Maryknoll, N.Y.: Orbis, 1977) and the author of *Politics and Ethics* (New York: Paulist, 1974).

Many Americans who involve themselves in foreign policy debates are puzzled by the sudden appearance in their midst of the National Conference of Catholic Bishops (NCCB), whose past political activism had been confined largely to the issues of abortion and support for private education. How have the Bishops come to thrust themselves into the intricacies of the debate about nuclear strategy and arms control?

Such resistance to governmental policies is not altogether new to the American Catholic hierarchy, which became a prominent political actor after the 1973 Supreme Court decision on abortion. In their struggle to reverse the momentum of public support on this issue, the Bishops have gained political sophistication and a sense of solidarity. Indeed, some commentators believe that it was the Bishops' high profile in the abortion debate which led them, somewhat to their own surprise, into the midst of the national debate about defense policy.[1] For the Bishops' conspicuous advocacy of the right to life for the unborn made imperative an equally spirited campaign to reverse the momentum of nuclear escalation. By remaining silent on the moral repugnance of the doctrine of assured destruction, the Bishops seemed to be condoning this comprehensive and perhaps ultimate threat to human life.

Background: Vatican II and Senate Testimony

Influential in steering the Bishops toward an explicit treatment of the morality of nuclear deterrence has been a growing faction within the hierarchy itself, comprising Bishops associated with the American branch of Pax Christi, an international Catholic peace movement that groups together both pacifists and those who hold more traditional Catholic views on the justifiability of war. The impact of this group on the Bishops' public posture was first noticeable in 1979 in the testimony presented by John Cardinal Krol, Archbishop of Philadelphia, before the U.S. Senate Foreign Relations Committee hearings on the SALT II arms control agreements.[2]

The Cardinal came bearing tidings from his fellow U.S. Bishops, who were then beginning to exercise their new charter, bestowed by the Second Vatican Council, as an autonomous teaching authority within the Church.[3] Wearing the new mantle of collegiality—the authority invested in national conferences of bishops to address the moral problems of particular concern to various nations—Krol communicated to the Senate Committee the NCCB's official, but qualified, support for SALT II. He likewise presented a radical challenge to the present U.S. nuclear strategy, which remains essentially unhampered by the modest restrictions on weapons systems required by the now dormant treaty. In developing his testimony for the Committee, the Cardinal relied heavily on the treatment of nuclear deterrence which had been developed by Vatican II. And yet, crucial passages in his own testimony also reflected the special anxieties of the American Bishops and represented a critical advance beyond the position on deterrence adopted by the Vatican Council.

It is not surprising that the American Church took the lead in the postconciliar Church by challenging nuclear deterrence. For not only is the United States the only nation ever to have used atomic weapons in war, but it is also the only superpower open to religious influence. The morality of nuclear deterrence is preeminently (although by no means exclusively) an American problem. And hence the present leadership of the American Church is attempting to bring to the consciousness of the universal Church the witness of one nation's memory of having used atomic weapons against cities, of having committed the "unspeakable crime against God and man" which the Vatican Council had resoundingly condemned. The American churchmen had learned through experience to eschew reliance on the weapon with which the United States has permanently burdened the human condition. Memory is an unimpeachable moral witness.

Even if Cardinal Krol had merely brought to the attention of the Senators the strictures of Vatican II against the use of nuclear weapons, his testimony would have been weighty enough.[4] For, in its conciliar analysis, Vatican II relied on an ancient intellectual and moral tradition for assessing the moral legitimacy of the political use of force, namely, the "just war" tradition. Although the scholastic language in which it is presented often obscures the utility of such a moral calculus, the core of the theory lies in its straightforward attempt to reconcile two apparently conflicting human rights: the right to a just political order and the right to life.

Without the right to resort to force, citizens could easily become prey to injustice; tyrants and emperors would rule unchecked. Therefore, Catholic tradition reluctantly but resolutely affirms the moral acceptability of shedding blood in the name of justice: there is an inviolable right to revolution and to self-defense. These undeniable rights exist, however, in tension with the right to life, which is the moral claim of people to be spared the excesses latent in the use of force. Because the sword seems to have a law of its own, and often defies both aggressor and victim, a philosophical sheath has been painstakingly fashioned to protect the sacredness of life. No blood may be shed without a soul-searching scrutiny of the causes, motives, strategies, and consequences of any military action.

Both the exigencies of justice and the innate tendency of violence to escalate are recognized in the fragile moral code known as the just war doctrine. It establishes stringent conditions for the morally legitimate use of force: (1) only a national government is authorized to wage war; (2) a government may do so only when its people (or those of a defenseless ally) have been subjected to a violation of their legitimate national prerogatives, and only in order to redress such a grievance; (3) the means chosen by a government to wage such a war may not include intentional attack on civilians; (4) the damage prudently feared as a result of the military effort may not outweigh the benefits reasonably expected to be derived from it; and, finally, (5) no futile military actions, such as reprisals without military rationale, may be undertaken.[5]

In its evaluation of modern war according to the rigorous standards of the Church's own tradition, Vatican II went a long way toward challenging the legitimacy of the policy of assured destruction; it condemned all "indiscriminate" acts of war, that is, the deliberate "destruction of entire cities or of extensive areas along with their populations"—a strategy which the Council branded "a crime against God and man" which "merits unequivocal and unhesitating condemnation." Because any execution of the American deterrent threat would almost certainly include such acts—barring the implausible scenario of Soviet capitulation at a lower level of escalation—the Council's anathema certainly falls on present U.S. deterrence policy.

Although it warned that the continued deployment of gargantuan arsenals constitutes an apocalyptic risk that cannot be tolerated indefinitely, Vatican II stopped short of calling for unilateral nuclear disarmament; it prudently approved the continued maintenance of Western nuclear arsenals, while expressing urgent demands for progress in mutual and verifiable arms reductions. The Council thus lent its authority to a crucial distinction between the *use* of nuclear weapons against forbidden targets and continued *possession* of arsenals deployed for the purpose of wreaking exactly such civilian destruction. Continued possession of such arsenals at present was grudgingly approved as an inescapable condition of international security and arms control negotiations.

This crucial distinction likewise inspired the more radical stand that Cardinal Krol articulated on behalf of the American Bishops. His Senate testimony went significantly beyond the Vatican II strictures, because he condemned *all* use (or even threatened use) of strategic nuclear weapons against any targets whatsoever. The majority of the American Bishops were opposed to the use of strategic weapons even against military targets, and seemed to have anticipated much of the current public questioning of the feasibility of controlling the scale of nuclear exchanges.[6]

In his statement, Cardinal Krol continuously reverted to the question of the uncontrollability of nuclear war. When government officials absolve themselves of the requirement to use force to accomplish some reasonable political purpose, he insisted, they relinquish any claim to justifying their resort to force.[7] Even in modern times, war, unlike some of its contemporary instruments, cannot guide itself: it needs the hand of political power to succeed. Abandoning the determination to provide such guidance is an abdication of political responsibility because it risks trading the security of the people for an empty display of "national" resolve or vindictiveness.[8] Against such a betrayal of the people, the Church raises a voice of protest.

Development of the Pastoral Letter

Cardinal Krol's appearance before the Senate committee in support of SALT II signaled the U.S. Catholic hierarchy's decision to speak out on the morality of deterrence. His testimony went virtually unnoticed, but the Bishops' subsequent initiatives in challenging nuclear strategy have drawn increasing attention and even caused considerable alarm in some quarters. For, as they entered into an elaborate process of consultation with public officials (and other specialists) on the intricacies of the political, military, technological, and moral dimensions of the arms race, the Bishops have been unable to escape public attention.

In June 1982, after six months of public hearings, a committee of five Bishops, chaired by Cardinal Joseph Bernardin, Archbishop of Chicago, circulated a first draft of the proposed Pastoral Letter to all those they had consulted, as well as to their fellow Bishops, asking for suggested revisions of the text. They were not disappointed; they were eventually inundated with 700 pages of criticisms and suggestions. After reviewing these comments, they released a second draft of the letter in late October 1982.

This second version came as something of a shock because, despite the vigorous public objections of Reagan Administration officials, the drafting committee made the proposed evaluation of nuclear deterrence more restrictive than that contained in the earlier document. They condemned *all* nuclear war, eliminating the tolerance for some counterforce strategies that earlier had been judged acceptable.

The revised statement, prepared for the 1982 annual meeting of the Bishops, included the following features: (1) condemnation of any use (or even threatened use) of the U.S. strategic arsenal against cities, or against vast areas with their populations; (2) a similar condemnation of its use against military targets located near population centers; (3) prohibition of first use of nuclear weapons against any targets; and, finally, (4) prohibition of any use of nuclear weapons that might escape human control. All these restrictions on the use (or threat of use) of nuclear weapons were summed up in the words: "We must continually say 'no' to the idea of nuclear war."[9] In addition, the Bishops recommended: a nuclear freeze (immediate, bilateral verifiable agreements to halt testing, production, and deployment of new strategic systems); negotiated bilateral "deep cuts" in the arsenals of both superpowers; and a comprehensive test-ban treaty.

Along with toleration for maintaining the arsenal itself at the present level, pending bilateral reductions, the Pastoral Letter recommends an increase of conventional forces in order to provide strategic alternatives to reliance on nuclear weapons. Sympathetic to the imperatives of national security, the Bishops have lent the weight of their authority to the search for an alternative policy that will enhance the present deterrent force by providing a more credible but less morally repugnant defense policy.

Of all the passages in the Pastoral Letter, the strangest one for most Americans may well be the following:

> We remind all in authority and in the chain of command that their training and field manuals have long prohibited, and still do prohibit, certain actions in the conduct of war, especially those actions which inflict harm on innocent civilians. The question is not whether certain measures are unlawful or forbidden in warfare, but which measures: to refuse to take such actions is not an act of cowardice or treason but one of courage and patriotism.[10]

The Bishops are serious indeed about their challenge to deterrence strategy, even going so far as to forbid Catholic officers to participate in certain integral functions of the present deterrent strategy, such as attacking civilian centers. And this indirect intervention in the nation's foreign policy has evoked the alarm of commentators unfamiliar with the Catholic tradition in politics.

The Bishops' challenge, however, should have come as no surprise. For over a millennium, the Church has sought to hobble wayward governments in just this fashion, by denying them the personnel necessary to carry out unwarranted military campaigns. Not content simply to counsel the king against unwarranted use of force, the Church has also spoken to his subordinates and commanded them to lay down their arms.[11] After denying the competence of the state to wage war at the unjust whim of the prince, the Church also seeks to sap his strength by denying him the instrument of military policy indispensable even in the nuclear era—skilled warriors. But the Church is not inadvertently subversive. Its genius is to furnish the spiritual leverage required to divert any government whose unswerving policy is inimical to the welfare of the people. There are, the Bishops believe, things the state may not do. Because the people have an inalienable right to life, liberty, and the pursuit of happiness, the government's military competence is limited to fashioning security policies compatible with the survival and well-being of the people.

This intransigence in criticizing security policies arises from a worldview that has taken shape over two millennia and that rests on a minimalist view of the state. In the eyes of the Catholic Church, the legitimate role of government is limited by the competing rights of other, nongovernmental members of society, including the individual, the family, and the Church itself. The person is prior—in his individuality as well as in his chosen associations—to the state. It is precisely this priority— metaphysical and moral—which established the tradition of inalienable rights delimiting the competence of the state. Secure within this tradition, the Church feels confident in challenging the state's competence to order citizens to support or execute military policies that the Church views as irremediably perverse.

In setting out to encourage a profound shift in defense policy, the Bishops are thus calling on Americans (and implicitly the churches and citizens of their allies, especially in the NATO nations) to capitalize on the distinctive resources of the West, both material and spiritual. Their summons to explore alternative defense postures is animated by the conviction that the technological advantage enjoyed by Western nations provides a margin of maneuver which can now be exploited to avert a nuclear confrontation. The decisive appeal, however, is a spiritual challenge. The Bishops call on their fellow citizens to pause and reassess present U.S. defense policies in the light of Western political tradition, which prides itself on the observance of certain limits on the use of power, and on the insistence, for example, that some military strategies violate human instincts that control the use of violence. Especially because the U.S. Bishops understand that the present, and undoubtedly perduring, struggle between East and West is precisely a struggle between competing cultures, they insist that this struggle cannot be won with a display of superior force alone. Only by bringing to bear one of the distinctive strengths of Western culture—its respect for conscience as the guide of politics—will the West "prevail" in this struggle in any sense worthy of itself. The West, while it remains itself, will continue to draw the line at genocide. When it steps across that line, as it now routinely and unthinkingly threatens to do by unleashing its nuclear deterrent force, the fundamental struggle will have ended, no matter which side "prevails" in the ensuing battle. Heading off such a cultural capitulation is the mission the Bishops seem to have chosen for themselves at this moment in history.

Political Impact

How should one estimate the chances that the Bishops will succeed in this mission? The auspices are good, but not without some disturbing signs.

The most promising recent development is the shift of focus in the public debate to the "no first use" campaign (which has brought together an improbable coalition of critics of present nuclear strategy). Initiatives such as these run parallel to a central emphasis of the Bishops' Pastoral Letter which condemns present NATO strategy to be the first to use nuclear weapons in the event of aggression.

Apparently without coordination, various individuals and groups have made remarkably consonant attacks on the longstanding NATO policy of relying on nuclear weapons to redress the conventional military imbalance in Europe. The most prominent of these challenges to NATO policy was that laid down by four American statesmen—including some of the original architects of the present U.S. strategy—McGeorge Bundy, George Kennan, Robert McNamara, and Gerard Smith. Their article in *Foreign Affairs*, "Nuclear Weapons and the Atlantic Alliance,"[12] gave voice to widespread attitudes among American specialists in political-military affairs when they expressed concern about the risks inherent in a policy that includes NATO's threat to use nuclear weapons in response to conventional aggression by the Warsaw Pact. Arguing that the present strategic parity between the United States and the Soviet Union makes such a reliance on the inherently escalatory employment of nuclear weapons at once less credible and more threatening to U.S. security, Bundy et al. urge a renewed examination of the option to renounce first use of nuclear weapons in Europe. They concede that a dramatic reversal of NATO policy would have to await the enhancement of the conventional NATO force structure, but plead for such a policy reversal on grounds of political realism. The present policy, they insist, can result either in idle and deceptive threats of hemispheric destruction or, worse still, in the execution of such a scheme. In the new era of strategic parity, what the present policy cannot conceivably accomplish is the defense of Europe, only the possibility of its destruction.

This thoughtful (and, because of the stature of its authorship, potentially persuasive) article pleads for a reintegration of deterrence policy with defense planning. Deterrence—which has traditionally been the fruit of sound defense planning, achieving the goals of defense without paying the price of war—has gradually become separated from defense policy. Persuaded that deterrence would be more secure insofar as its failure would unleash destructive forces that mock the notion of defense, recent military policy has unwisely accepted a dichotomy between deterrence and defense. The authors of the *Foreign Affairs* article call for a reintegration of these two complementary dimensions of security policy, deterrence, and defense. Deterrence should rest on the credible potential to use military force in a way that would not inevitably annihilate the society seeking to defend itself. Rejecting the modern dichotomy between deterrence and defense, Bundy et al. revert to the traditional policy of deploying usable military forces to deter aggression.

The consensus emerging among influential critics of the present policy of first use of nuclear weapons in the European theatre is initially encouraging. Yet, not a single prominent American official or political candidate has endorsed these initiatives to undertake a reassessment of deterrence policy. Expert opinion, perhaps not surprisingly, appears to be markedly ahead of the American political debate on this point: the most challenging voices endorse the freeze movement but leave unexamined the present policy of planned first use of the nuclear arsenal. Political discourse thus continues to accept complacently the disjunction between deterrence and defense.

There is hope that a bold presidential candidate in 1984 (or, at the latest, in 1988) will adopt the "no first use" platform in a bid for the presidency and thereby shift the focus of national debate. For the campaign to eschew the first use of nuclear weapons has been careful to insist that such a policy reversal would not undermine deterrence. NATO would still retain the policy of nuclear retaliation if the Warsaw Pact chose to utilize nuclear weapons itself. Although it makes the resort to nuclear weapons by NATO markedly less probable (because of the upgrading of conventional defense), the proposed policy revision unambiguously supports the continued deterrent threat of retaliatory use of the strategic nuclear arsenal. Because Bundy et al. confine their challenge to resisting NATO's first use of nuclear weapons, their proposals remain within the familiar landscape of post-World War II defense policy. Their initiative is simply an effort to adjust that policy to the new realities of European economic and technological recovery, on the one hand, and the emergence of strategic parity between the superpowers, on the other. Political candidates can be expected to learn to speak this language of moderate reform in security policy.

The Bishops, however, might as well be speaking Latin. For they are proposing a radical reversal of a generation of policy in which security rests on the threat of assured destruction. The Bishops are pleading for a shift to "no first use" of nuclear weapons, but they do not stop there. They also condemn retaliatory use of these weapons: "We must say 'no' to nuclear war." The Bishops' challenge to national policy can be adequately described only as radical.

Is the Pastoral Letter, therefore, politically irrelevant? Have the Bishops moved so far from the center of political discourse that their voices will be inaudible? Has their commitment to moral purity condemned them to political irrelevance? Any answer to these questions depends on the persuasiveness of the Bishops' conviction that retention of the nuclear arsenal constitutes a (stabilizing) deterrent factor even apart from the declaration (or intention) to use the arsenal in retaliation for prior use by the Soviet Union. The Bishops' resistance to the notion of unilateral dismantling of the nuclear arsenal derives from their conviction that, even apart from a policy of retaliation, the arsenal deters aggression. This belief seems to rest on the perception that a U.S. policy to renounce retaliatory use of the arsenal, coupled with the maintenance of the arsenal itself, would be dismissed by the Soviets as a merely (and perversely deceptive) declaratory policy adopted for propaganda purposes. Soviet planners would look to the recommended enhancement of conventional forces, in addition to the tolerated maintenance of the nuclear arsenal, as evidence of heightened preparedness for waging all-out war. Hence, the Bishops seem to believe that their recommended reorientation of deterrence strategy would not undermine deterrence. The increased credibility of the use of conventional force in, for example, Europe might even enhance deterrence.

In proposing an alternative formula for deterrence which is more credible than the present defense posture because it is consonant with the moral and political instincts of the American people, the Bishops have inaugurated a vigorous national security debate. The letter had been dismissed by editorialists and criticized by strategists. At the same time it has been welcomed by others, no less experienced in the management of national security affairs, as a thoughtful initiative. McGeorge Bundy, for example, praises their formula for "existential deterrence" as a step away from the brink of nuclear war which does not signal a retreat from America's commitment to the common security.[13] These contradictory reviews of the Pastoral Letter reflect divergent perspectives on the dynamics of deterrence in the nuclear era. Those who welcome the proposal for "existential deterrence" (including many senior military officers, strategic analysts and national intelligence community officials whom the present author has consulted) agree with the Bishops that Soviet planners, faced with the shift of national security policy proposed by the Bishops, would base their threat estimates on the arsenal being retained rather than on the policy being enunciated. Given the structure of U.S.-USSR perceptions, such a skeptical dismissal of the (hypothetically adopted) shift of U.S. defense policy would be inevitable. Soviet officials would continue to stand in dread of the destructive capacity inherent in the nuclear arsenal even when it is severed from the policy of use. For such a (hypothetical) policy of "use, never" could be instantaneously reversed by the president with no more formality than a call for the "football" (the nuclear-code case that is always at his side).

Deterrence, in other words, is in the eye of the beholder. The test to be passed by any formula for deterrence is not, as some mathematically oriented strategists seem to assume, whether "nation x" and "nation y" can be deterred by the presence of ready arsenals whose use has been foresworn. Rather it is whether these two specific nations, the United States and the Soviet Union, would be reliably deterred in this paradoxical posture. Those who welcome the Pastoral Letter's formula for deterrence are convinced that, like the Soviet's oft-repeated disclaimer of the intention to be the first to use nuclear weapons, an American self-denying declaratory policy would be given short shrift by the adversary.

Therefore, while the Pastoral Letter urges a radical reorientation of defense strategy, it rejects the precipitous reversal of security arrangements entailed in any effort to bring about unilateral nuclear disarmament. It settles for a deterrent policy that combines a conventional force ready for use in certain circumstances with a nuclear force whose use has been renounced. Such a combination of factors, they judge, is the necessary and sufficient condition of security in the nuclear age. Nothing less is adequate to defend our security; nothing more is militarily required nor morally acceptable.

The Pastoral Letter's formula for a reorientation of deterrence is thus exceptionally subtle: radical without being precipitous. Its possible contribution to the public debate will, however, be determined by its plausibility. If the public, uneasy with the risks inherent in present policy but equally cautious in seeking alternative security arrangements, displays a like subtlety of analysis of the requirements (and limits) of deterrence policy in the nuclear age, then the surprising, "realistic" radicalism of the Bishops may help to shape a new American consensus on defense policy. Subtlety, however, has not always marked American public opinion on matters of defense. Its appearance now in a favorable reception to the Pastoral Letter would be a sign of a growing public awareness that "deterrence as usual" will not do. Desperation may be the mother of subtlety. Without such subtlety, the people may sense, they will perish.

Conclusion

Do Bishops ever have doubts? Presumably, in this instance, they are wondering whether their solution to the nuclear impasse may not be too subtle, too akin to the calculations of power politics. They have called for increases in conventional military preparedness and have endorsed the maintenance of the nuclear arsenal until verifiable reductions can be negotiated between the superpowers. Are they not conceding too much to the imperatives of this world and retreating from their own proper perspective?

When they experience these doubts, the Bishops must be relieved to recall a passage from Christ's instructions to his disciples, included in the Sermon on the Mount (Matthew 10:16):

> Remember, I am sending you out like sheep among wolves; be as wise as serpents, as innocent as doves.

If ever a group of Christian leaders have fulfilled that paradoxical evangelical mandate, it is the American Catholic Bishops in their present subtle appeal for a profound, but not precipitous, reorientation of national security policy. Surely, their hopes rest in the judgment that the public mind in America is no less subtle than theirs, no less wise and no less innocent.

NOTES

This essay is a slightly revised version of an article which appeared in *Science, Technology and Human Values*, vol. 8, issue 3 (Summer 1983), and is reprinted with permission of the Massachusetts Institute of Technology and the President and Fellows of Harvard College. Copyright © 1983 by John Wiley & Sons, Inc. Reprinted by permission of the publisher.

1. Kenneth A. Briggs, "The Bishops' United Front," *Christian Century*, vol. 98, no. 41 (16 December 1981), pp. 1301–02.

2. U.S. Senate, Committee on Foreign Relations, The SALT II Treaty, Hearings on EX Y, 96-1, 96th Congress, First Session, 1979, Part IV, pp.116–30.

3. Collegial sharing of authority among the bishops of the world, especially through the instrument of national or regional conferences of bishops, is authorized in the Decree on the Bishops' Pastoral Office in the Church. The English text is found in Walter M. Abbott, S.J., and Joseph Gallagher, eds., *The Documents of Vatican II* (New York: America Press, 1966), pp. 396–429.

4. *The Documents of Vatican II*, "The Church in the Modern World," nos. 78–82, pp. 290–97.

5. Representative surveys of the history and theology of the just war tradition include: Frederick H. Russell, *The Just War in the Middle Ages* (Cambridge, England: Cambridge University Press, 1975); Paul Ramsey, *War and Christian Conscience* (Durham, N.C.: Duke University Press, 1961); Paul Ramsey, *The Just War: Force and Political Responsibility* (New York: Charles Scribner's Sons, 1968); James. T. Johnson, *Ideology, Reason and the Limitation of War* (Princeton, N.J.: Princeton University Press, 1975); James T. Johnson, *Just War Tradition and the Restraint of War: A Moral and Historical Inquiry* (Princeton, N.J.: Princeton University Press, 1981); LeRoy B. Walters, *Five Classic Just-War Theories* (Ph.D. dissertation, Yale University, 1971); William V. O'Brien, *War and/or Survival* (Garden City, N.Y.: Doubleday, 1969); William V. O'Brien, *The Conduct of Just and Limited War* (New York: Praeger, 1981).

6. John D. Steinbruner, "Nuclear Decapitation," *Foreign Policy*, no. 45 (Winter 1981–82), pp. 16–28. For a government document summarizing diffidence about continuing government control of nuclear war, see Harold Brown, *Department of Defense Annual Report*, FY1981 (21 January 1980), p. 61.

7. Former Secretary of State Alexander Haig articulated this policy of abdication of governmental responsibility in an address at Georgetown University on 6 April 1982. "Flexible response is not premised upon the view that nuclear war can be controlled. Every successive allied and American government has been convinced that a nuclear war, once initiated, could escape such control. They have therefore agreed upon a strategy which retains the deterrent effect of a possible nuclear response, without making such a step in any sense automatic."

8. It seems indeed that the government is presently prepared to countenance such a development. Admitting the possibility of "nuclear decapitation" in the opening phases of a nuclear exchange (which would likely leave national command centers hors de combat due to the electromagnetic effects of nuclear detonations), government officials nonetheless are steeling themselves for the decision to let control of any ensuing escalation devolve upon the ranks of subordinate commanders who are irreparably severed from contact with the national command center, with one another, or with any reliable information about military and

political developments in the Soviet Union. In such a scenario, any pretensions the government may have had to calibrate hostilities to ensure the immunity of civilians or the preponderance of benefits over costs will have been exploded.

9. National Conference of Catholic Bishops, *The Challenge of Peace: God's Promise and Our Response* (Washington, D.C.: United States Catholic Conference, 1983), II, D2, 188. A categorical formulation is found in II, A, 132: " . . . we must reject nuclear war." See also II, A, 131, 138; B, 140; D2, 175.

10. *Ibid.,* IV, C, 311.

11. Cf. Frederick H. Russell, *op. cit.,* esp. pp. 151–55.

12. McGeorge Bundy, George Kennan, Robert McNamara, and Gerard Smith, "Nuclear Weapons and the Atlantic Alliance," *Foreign Affairs,* vol. 60, no. 4 (Spring 1982), pp. 753–68; Independent Commission on Disarmament and Security Issues (Chairman Olof Palme), *Common Security* (New York: Simon and Schuster, 1983), pp. 107–18; Jonathan Dean, "Beyond First Use," *Foreign Policy,* no. 48 (Fall 1982), pp. 37–53; *No First Use,* A Report by the Union of Concerned Scientists (Cambridge, Mass.: 1 February 1983), endorsed by numerous political and military leaders of NATO nations, 70 pp.; and finally, the Report of the European Security Study, *Strengthening Conventional Deterrence in Europe* (New York: St. Martin's Press, 1983).

13. McGeorge Bundy has coined this phrase to delineate the distinctive doctrine of deterrence fashioned by the Bishops, employing the phrase in his essay "The Bishops and the Bomb," *The New York Review of Books,* vol. 30, no. 10 (June 16, 1983), pp. 3–8. Less enthusiastic responses to various drafts of the Letter may be found in: "The Bishops and the Bomb," *The New York Times,* May 6, 1983 (A30); "In Defense of Deterrence," *The New Republic,* vol. 187, no. 24 (December 20, 1982), p. 7. A strategist's lament may be found in Albert Wohlstetter, "Bishops, Statesmen, and Other Strategists," *Commentary,* vol. 75, no. 6 (June 1983), pp. 18–35.

WILLIAM V. O'BRIEN

The Challenge of War: A Christian Realist Perspective

William V. O'Brien is chairman and Professor of Government, Georgetown University, the author of *The Conduct of Just and Limited War* (1981), and a consultant to the U.S. Bishops Ad Hoc Committee that drafted *The Challenge of Peace*.

The American Catholic Bishops' 1983 Pastoral Letter on War and Peace, *The Challenge of Peace: God's Promise and Our Response,* is a flawed document.[1] Most efforts to apply Christian moral values to complex policy issues may be expected to have deficiencies and ambiguities. However, when such efforts are flawed from the outset by their approach to the empirical and moral problems addressed, the consequences of their deficiencies and ambiguities are particularly grave and pervasive. This is the case with the Pastoral Letter. Indeed, the problem with the Bishops' approach begins with the title. The subject should really be "The Challenge of War."

The moral issues of war are about legitimate ends and means of armed coercion employed in the defense of life, liberty, justice and peace itself. Although armed force has shaped our history and political geography and is the foundation of whatever domestic and international security we enjoy, discussion of the moral issues of its employment is unpleasant and often baffling. Thus, while the moral issues of recourse to armed force are unavoidable, they are somehow avoided, particularly by those professing the greatest interest in the moral dimensions of public affairs. The perennial fate of discussions of the morality of war is to be sidetracked into more edifying subjects such as the moral obligation to remove the supposed causes of war or to outline blueprints for a world without war. Regrettably, the American Catholic Bishops have succumbed to the temptation to change the subject of the morality of war to that of the morality of seeking a world without war, as indicated by their Pastoral Letter's title, "The Challenge of Peace."

Those familiar with the 1983 Pastoral Letter may object, at this point, that the document seems to be mainly concerned with issues of nuclear deterrence and war, and that it is inaccurate and unfair to charge the Bishops with changing the subject from war to peace. However, it will be the contention of this chapter that the Bishops, having marched up to the great issues of deterrence and war, flinched at the critical moment and begged the questions that they had raised about these issues. They then beat a retreat into the more uplifting world of progress in arms control. This progress, it is thought, will lead to the elimination of the causes of war through the banishment of the arms race and the accompanying reallocation of resources and human genius to solving the economic and social problems that supposedly bar the way to the realization of true peace.

There is a need to address these problems of international economic and social justice and the Church does, indeed, address them frequently and passionately. However, there is also a need to address the problems of war and, having done so, to stick to the task until the best possible guidance has been formulated. The American Catholic Bishops' 1983 Pastoral Letter accords the problems of deterrence and war an extremely lengthy analysis, reflecting an extrordinary drafting effort, but it abandons the enterprise at the critical point. The Bishops leave the faithful and the interested public, as well as themselves, with serious unfinished business.

Surely the central point of the Bishops' inquiry was the judgment as to the moral permissibility of using nuclear weapons. While it is abundantly clear that they condemn such use on moral and practical grounds, they never reach a final, definitive, explicit statement on this question. Accordingly, they never close with the critical issue of deterrence, namely, "Can you threaten what you would not do morally?" Instead, the Bishops leave this question, in the formulation of their principal technical adviser, Father J. Bryan Hehir, shrouded in a "centimeter of ambiguity."[2] Such an elusive and coy characterization of moral guidance on a subject of staggering import is surely extraordinary but it errs, if at all, only in the number of centimeters that are required to measure the various ambiguities of the Pastoral Letter. The analysis that follows will attempt to identify these deficiencies and ambiguities with respect to the ends and means of nuclear deterrence.

Idealism and Realism in Morality and Politics

Translated into the terms of the basic approaches to politics and political morality, whether domestic or international, the Bishops in their 1983 Pastoral Letter venture out of their customary idealism, confront the moral and practical dilemmas of deterrence and defense in the nuclear age in a manner reflecting at least some elements of a realist approach, and then slam the door on realism, returning to the preferred realm of idealism. This characterization is not intended to imply that idealists are always unrealistic or misguided any more than that realists are necessarily realistic and wise. It is to suggest that in their latest venture into the realm of war morality the American Catholic Bishops found themselves suspended between their habitual idealism and an uncharacteristic realism. The result is that realism faltered and idealism triumphed in a way that essentially vitiated the Bishops' brief excursion into realist analysis.

It is not necessary to reconstruct the whole classic idealist-realist debate that dominates political and moral approaches to policy issues. However, the present debate on the morality of nuclear deterrence and war has been profoundly affected by the consequences of the idealist-realist dichotomy and a brief review of the subject is in order. Idealists and realists differ on three interrelated issues: human nature, the nature of politics, and the role of armed force in politics. From an optimistic view of the perfectibility of human nature, the idealist sees politics primarily as the resolution of problems through enlightened reason and cooperation, with little, if any, need to introduce armed coercion to assure law, order and justice. The realist, starting with a pessimistic view of human nature, sees politics as the balancing of competing interests to produce a tolerable minimal consensus enforced, when necessary, by armed coercion.[3]

These are generalizations, of course, and most of us mix and vary the elements of idealism and realism in our political views and actions. Nevertheless, the direction of the emphases in each approach is important, particularly in international politics where there is no central authority to enforce law and order, much less justice. Idealists tend to view armed force not even as a necessary evil but as an unnecessary evil. That is to say, force may be tolerated as a necessary evil pending the day when more progress has been made in establishing an international political system based on reason and cooperation. Even so, it is thought that armed force often is far more "evil" than "necessary," to the point that some idealists view it as a literally unnecessary evil.[4] This is a critical issue that is at the heart of the failure of the American Catholic Bishops and many morally concerned Christians and men and women of good will to come to grips with the moral issues of war. For them, it is not simply that war is evil and destructive. The crowning tragedy is that war is unnecessary, *viz.*, there never was a good war or a bad peace. In modern times this view has often been given the gloss of psychological and psychiatric specialists who explain confidently that war is a product of mental illness.[5] It is, of course, difficult to defend, much less promote, much less formulate the moral principles of, mental illness.

Realists, on the other hand, differ among themselves over the extent of evil to be imputed to war as an instrument of policy while agreeing generally that it is necessary. There are those who would hold that war may be more properly viewed, in some circumstances, as a good rather than an evil. In any event, realist approaches to international politics differ from idealist ones most significantly on the issue of the necessity and perennial character of recourse to armed force as a characteristic of international interaction.

The realist component in the American Catholic Bishops' 1983 Pastoral Letter is based on a reaffirmation of traditional just war doctrine. This, at least, is an achievement (not to have been lightly assumed) for which Christian realists are grateful. In the 1983 Pastoral Letter, the Bishops do not simply brush aside the problems of international security in the manner of many official Catholic pronouncements, and they do not preempt the discussion of the moral issues of deterrence and defense with an early introduction of pleas to change the international system into something different wherein war has no place.

However, the promise held out by the early reassertion of the just war doctrine as the authoritative source of guidance for analyses of the morality of war is not realized in the 1983 Pastoral Letter. This is the case because the Bishops do not follow the full just war doctrine and methodology in their analyses of nuclear deterrence and defense. They alter the sequence and the comparative weight of the elements of just war analyses so substantially as to fail to subject the subject of nuclear deterrence and war to a thorough, comprehensive just war evaluation.

Just war doctrine addresses the decision to go to war, the *jus ad bellum*, war-decision law.[6] Then it addresses the war-conduct law, the *jus in bello*. In basic terms, just war doctrine provides standards for judging the ends and means of war. In my view, the American Catholic Bishops, in their 1983 Pastoral Letter, only belatedly and inadequately mention the ends of nuclear deterrence and defense. Their discussion of war is almost exclusively an exercise in the morality of means, divorced from the ends that are the sole warrant for even considering the means in question. Inevitably, a discussion of means so portentous as nuclear deterrence and defense without a serious exploration of the putative ends for which such means are prepared is destined to be inadequate. Moreover, even within its own terms, the discussion of the means of nuclear deterrence and defense in the 1983 Pastoral Letter is deficient and ambiguous in that it does not even explicitly answer its own ultimate question of the moral permissibility of nuclear weapons.

In this chapter I will, first, explore the gap in the Pastoral Letter with regard to identification of threats to just causes that alone could justify even provisional endorsement of a means so dangerous as nuclear deterrence and defense. Second, I will show that the analysis of nuclear deterrence in the Bishops' Pastoral Letter is either incomplete and/or deliberately ambiguous to the point that it does not provide clear and helpful guidance to those who share responsibility for the defense of the free world and for their constituents. This critique will be offered from the standpoint of a Christian realist.

What Is the Just Cause Warranting Nuclear Deterrence and Defense?

The just war war-decision law requires that a number of conditions be met in order to overcome the moral presumption against recourse to armed force. These conditions are variously formulated by authorities. I incorporate them within the three conditions propounded by St. Thomas Aquinas, *viz.*, competent authority, just cause and right intention, by subsuming a number of the conditions under the general category of just cause, as follows:

(1) the comparative justice of the party claiming a just cause vis-à-vis the adversary;

(2) the just cause or causes themselves in the sense of *casus belli*, in modern just war doctrine and international law almost exclusively individual and collective self-defense;

(3) proportionality of the cost of defending the just cause to the good of defending it in the light of the probability of success;

(4) exhaustion of peaceful alternatives to protection of the just cause by resort to armed coercion.[7]

Every element in the just war doctrine is important and, in principle, every element must be substantially satisfied in order to warrant acceptance of recourse to armed coercion as morally permissible. That is not to say that a belligerent's record of compliance with just war conditions must be perfect in order to qualify a war as just. Some failures to meet just war standards, particularly in the conduct of the war, may be overcome by an overall record of compliance with both war-decision and war-conduct requirements. However, it is clear that nothing is warranted unless the putative just cause is established. Everything done in war refers to the necessity of defending the just cause. Nothing is warranted that cannot be shown to be necessary to the defense of the just cause.[8]

It is not a matter of pedantic methodology, therefore, to insist that a just war analysis address the war-decision law issues, the just cause issues, before turning to the war-conduct issues. To be sure, one can imagine means so hopelessly evil as to be *mala in se*, e.g., genocide. But not even "nuclear deterrence" and "nuclear war" are self-evidently *mala in se*. Certain forms of nuclear deterrence and nuclear war may be shown to be *mala in se*. However, unless it can be shown that all forms of nuclear deterrence and war must necessarily be included in the category of means that are wrong in themselves, means that are not proper for any cause, no matter how just, then it is not possible to go very far in evaluating the moral permissibility of nuclear force without reference to the just causes in defense of which nuclear force might be used.

The concept of proportionality is central both to war-decision and war-conduct law. The very decision to engage in war requires a calculus of the proportionality of the cost of the means to the end protected in the light of the probability of success. Obviously, this calculus requires a referent, an end to which the means must be proportionate. Every decision of military necessity in war-conduct law requires proportionality to the proximate military end and, ultimately, to the just end of the war.

Accordingly, a competent just war analysis of the present moral dilemmas of nuclear deterrence and defense must begin with a statement of the just cause or causes in virtue of which states have established and maintain nuclear deterrence and defense. Such an analysis would then proceed to an estimate of the threats to those just causes. In view of the values at stake and the threats to those values, the moral permissibility of nuclear deterrence and defense would then be judged.

This was not, however, the approach of the American Catholic Bishops in their 1983 Pastoral Letter. The elements of just war doctrine are outlined in Part I.[9] But Part II, the heart of the Pastoral Letter, plunges immediately into a discussion of the morality of nuclear war that is marked from the outset by an emphasis on its extraordinary destructiveness. It is clear from the first paragraph of Part II on that nuclear war will be condemned as a practically catastrophic and morally unusable means without being considered in relation to the ends for which its use is threatened in deterrence.[10] There will be no calculus of proportionality of ends and means, only a peremptory judgment that no ends can justify such means, that nuclear deterrence and war are *mala in se*. It is clear from the first pages of Part II of the Pastoral Letter that nothing can be considered worse than the "dead" part of the "red or dead" dilemma that has haunted the free world since the 1940s. This is a plausible approach but it is not a just war approach. Just war judges means in relation, in proportion, to ends, not means in the abstract.

A just war approach would balance the risks of nuclear destruction with the risks of loss of freedom and fundamental rights that relinquishment of nuclear deterrence and defense would probably engender. It is not surprising that many secular humanists who oppose nuclear deterrence and war seem willing to risk the possibility, however remote it may appear to them, of loss of fundamental rights in order to preserve life. It is surprising, however, that representatives of a Church based on belief in a supernatural destiny for mankind should be inclined to place physical existence before fundamental freedoms, including the freedom to worship God. If this is an unfair criticism it is one that is invited by the fact that the American Catholic Bishops, given ample opportunity, choose not even to acknowledge the possible consequences for human freedom and rights if the protection of nuclear deterrence and defense is subverted, in part through their own efforts.

The Bishops address the issues of nuclear war with a "morality first" approach. That is to say, they put nuclear deterrence and defense through a moral analysis without reference to the necessity of these means to the defense of freedom and human rights, and come to the conclusion that nuclear deterrence and defense do not pass the test of moral permissibility.[11] Therefore, these means must, at most, be only temporarily condoned as a necessary evil and speedily eliminated. But this "morality first" approach is a stunted, incomplete, morality of means only approach. There is scarcely any recognition of the morality of ends and of the consequences to those ends that would be critically affected by a rigid application of the conclusions produced in the morality of means analysis.

Since the American Catholic Bishops are certainly not disposed consciously to put at risk the fundamental freedoms and values of the free world, how can one explain this failure to relate the consequences of any weakening of Western deterrence and defense to the prospects for that freedom and those values to survive? Some might suggest that the reason is that the Church, having allegedly erred on the side of excessive anti-Communism, is now seeking to alter its stand by downgrading the threat of Communist and other totalitarian aggressors to the free world. However, the more fundamental point would seem to be that suggested in the earlier discussion of idealist and realist approaches to politics.

The majority of the present generation of American Catholic Bishops appears to be committed to idealist attitudes toward recourse to armed force to the point of being doctrinaire on the subject. Their every impulse is to "say no to nuclear war," "say no to the arms race," "say no to defense spending that comes at the expense of the poor"—in brief, to "say no to war." There are still enough Bishops with realist propensities to defend just war doctrine but the majority of American Catholic Bishops appear to differ on the issue of recourse to armed force mainly to the extent that some consider it to be a necessary evil whereas a substantial minority considers it to be an unnecessary evil. To all of them, nuclear deterrence and defense, the arms race, defense spending, are a clear and present danger. Loss of freedom and fundamental human rights as the result of intimidation and aggression are not seen as clear and present dangers. Or so it would appear.

The fact is that the American Catholic Bishops, in the 1983 Pastoral Letter, launch into an extended discussion of nuclear deterrence and defense with little if any indication as to why such military preparations ever were or are now arguably necessary. Nuclear deterrence and defense are treated from the outset as something between a deadly disease and a pernicious habit. There is no estimate of the threats that might justify maintenance of nuclear deterrence and defense systems. There is not even a judgment that there are no threats, or that the threats are distant or marginal. In effect, the Bishops find that we are in a predicament caused by our development of nuclear military capabilities and that the sole issue is how to dismantle these capabilities in order to escape the predicament. What such a dismantling might do to the security of the free world is not a subject that interested the Bishops.

Given this approach, it is surprising that the American Catholic Bishops continue the approach of Vatican II and recent popes in condoning, however reluctantly and ambiguously, the temporary continuation of nuclear deterrence on condition that all possible efforts be made to eliminate nuclear weapons, the nuclear deterrence system and the arms race through arms control.[12] It is extraordinary for the Bishops to condone the deterrent because, given their manifest horror at the risks of nuclear war incurred by the perpetuation of the nuclear deterrence system, the logical conclusion would be that they would oppose continuation of deterrence. If there is no clear and present threat to free world liberty and values worth discussing in a pastoral letter on nuclear deterrence and defense, why tolerate the continued risks of nuclear deterrence another day?

The answer appears to be that the Bishops recognize that there are some threats, hence some need for a continued deterrent until arms control progress makes possible an end to the deterrent balance of terror and the arms race. But, since the Bishops do not offer any serious estimate either of the threats to freedom and human rights from potential nuclear aggressors or of the prospects for abating those threats, the rationale for continuing the nuclear deterrence system is fuzzy and implicit rather than explicit.

The closest that the 1983 Pastoral Letter comes to identifying the main threat that engenders Western nuclear deterrence and defense is in Part II.B.2, well after the analysis of the morality of nuclear deterrence and defense has been completed in Part II.[13] A section on "The Superpowers in a Disordered World," sandwiched in between a section on "World Order in Catholic Teaching" and one on "Interdependence: From Fact to Policy," touches briefly on some of the just cause issues. Obviously, it does not inform Part II very much either from the standpoint of the writing of Part II by the Bishops or the reading of the section by the faithful. Finally, however, on page twenty-five of a thirty-two-page version in *Origins*, the Pastoral Letter states:

> The fact of a Soviet threat, as well as the existence of a Soviet imperial drive for hegemony, at least in regions of major strategic interest, cannot be denied. The history of the Cold War has produced varying interpretations of which side caused the conflict, but whatever the details of history illustrate, the plain fact is that the memories of Soviet policies in Eastern Europe and recent events in Afghanistan and Poland have left their mark in the American political debate. Many people are forcibly kept under communist domination despite their manifest wishes to be free. Soviet power is very great. Whether the Soviet Union's pursuit of military might is motivated primarily by defensive or aggressive aims might be debated, but the effect is nevertheless to leave profoundly insecure those who must live in the shadow of that might.[14]

Before the contemporary Church was homogenized by secular humanism as it grappled with the political, economic and social issues of the day, there used to be great concern in Catholic circles about the pernicious effects of "relativism" and "value free" social sciences that were, in fact, not value free. To those who remember those concerns it is sadly ironic that the American Catholic Bishops cannot even compose a single paragraph explaining the threat of Soviet and other totalitarian aggression to the free world generally and the Church and its values in particular without "even-handed" statements that treat the causes of the threat with such clinical disinterestedness. One would be hard put to derive a just cause for free world deterrence and defense from the paragraph quoted.

Even supposing that the West might be as much at fault for the threat of war as the Soviet Union and its allies, or that the stakes between what is left of Christendom and the Communist world are unclear, important because "varying interpretations" have "left their mark in the American political debate," what is the opinion of the American Catholic Bishops, as distinct from the conventional wisdom of modern secular humanism, about the threat to free world and Christian values? Suppose, over time, the incredible happens and the Soviet Union and other Communist states take over much or all of the free world by intimidation and aggression. What would be the character of the regimes imposed? What, presumably, would be the consequences for the Christian faith? One would expect that to be a critical element in any analysis of just cause for nuclear deterrence and defense made by the episcopal leaders of the Roman Catholic Church in the Unitred States.

The Bishops provide an answer, however brief and indirect. They observe:

> Americans need have no illusions about the Soviet system of repression and the lack of respect in that system for human rights or about Soviet covert operations and pro-revolutionary activities. To be sure, our own system is not without flaws. Our government has sometimes supported repressive governments in the name of pre-serving freedom, has carried out repugnant covert operations of its own and remains imperfect in its domestic record of ensuring equal rights for all. At the same time there is a difference. NATO is an alliance of democratic countries which have freely chosen their association, the Warsaw Pact is not.[15]

One can extract from this somewhat rambling paragraph one sentence recognizing that the Soviet system is repressive and lacks respect for human rights. In the following paragraph, after some further even-handed admissions of American guilt and deficiencies, the Bishops' Pastoral Letter concedes that, whatever its faults:

> The facts simply do not support the invidious comparisons made at times even in our own society between our way of life, in which most basic human rights are at least recognized even if they are not always adequately supported, and those totalitarian and tyrannical regimes in which such rights are either denied or systematically sup-pressed. . . .[16]

This concession, however, is followed shortly by the admonition that:

> Insofar as this is true, however, it makes the promotion of human rights in our foreign policy, as well as our domestic policy, all the more important. It is the acid test of our commitment to our democratic values. In this light, any attempts to justify, for reasons of state, support for regimes that continue to violate human rights is all the more morally reprehensible in its hypocrisy.[17]

These statements can be read as an admonition to avoid allies with poor human rights records. Like the Soviet Union in World War II? Unfortunately, the geopolitics of collective defense against aggression do not always lead to alliances with Jeffersonian democracies. The paragraphs from which the quotations above are derived hardly put in perspective the critical just war issue at stake in nuclear deterrence and defense, namely, "What would the consequences be for Americans and their free world allies if they were conquered or reduced to dependencies by the Soviet Union, its allies or other totalitarian aggressors who would profit from the removal of our nuclear protection?"

Granted that the conquest of the United States and the principal free world countries is not a matter of immediate concern, particularly as long as nuclear deterrence and defense works, there are always targets for aggression at the periphery of the free world deterrence and defense systems. Each time they are threatened the issue is raised: Is their freedom worth the risks of nuclear deterrence and defense? Experience with past aggressors and the logic of collective deterrence/defense suggests that if this question is answered in the negative too many times it is likely that it will be raised with increasing frequency and closer to home. At bottom, the whole nuclear deterrence and defense system rests on the assumption that there is something so precious in the free world that its defense, even by the extreme and risky means of recourse to nuclear weapons, is morally justified.

Surely, no one reading the passages quoted above would have the remotest idea that the American Catholic Bishops consider the imposition by threat and use of armed force of Communist and other totalitarian tyrannies to be a just cause possibly warranting resistance with nuclear weapons. Put another way, the Bishops once again changed the subject. They changed the subject from the stakes in confrontations between the free and Communist worlds to the failings of what we call the free world, starting with our own and those of our allies. The moral of the story seems to be that we should worry more about human rights in South Korea, El Salvador and Egypt than about the threat to human rights in the countries that might have Gulag societies imposed upon them if U.S. deterrence and defense faltered.

Thus, while the morality of means analysis of the 1983 Pastoral Letter is dominated from beginning to end by worst case assumptions about nuclear war,[18], the tiny and belated effort to acknowledge the just causes at stake in modern international conflict is dominated with concerns about the quality of human rights in the countries that may fall victim to Communist and other aggressors. In these circumstances, it is not surprising that the Bishops can conclude that the moral presumptions are all against those who would rely on nuclear war to defend the freedom and rights of the free world. The possibility that the presumptions might go the other way, against those who would risk a dark age of Gulag societies rather than nuclear war in any form, is not even acknowledged, much less debated.[19] It appears from the American Catholic Bishops' 1983 Pastoral Letter that, after one has brushed aside the "centimeter of ambiguity," there is no just cause for nuclear deterrence and defense.

This means that the whole free world deterrence/defense system would collapse like a house of cards if the American Catholic Bishops' advice were followed. There patently is no serious nonnuclear defense against a nuclear aggressor unencumbered by moral scruples about using nuclear weapons. Beyond that, prospects for deterrence and defense on behalf of the free world may quickly be reduced to underground resistance, with hopes that it is more successful than in, say, the Soviet Union, Poland, Cuba, or the Peoples Republic of China. Beyond that, there is always the option of nonviolent resistance under circumstances considerably less propitious than those that confronted Mahatma Gandhi or Martin Luther King, Jr. Beyond that, there is always martyrdom. If these reflections seem melodramatic let it be recalled what Europe looked like after Hitler's successful conquests and before the United Nations rescued the peoples who did not realize the threats to their lives and liberties until it was too late.

Can a Bluff Deterrent Work until Nuclear Weapons Are Eliminated?

Without having made a serious estimate of the threats to free world liberties that might possibly explain the necessity for nuclear deterrence and defense, the American Catholic Bishops undertook a morality of means analysis of nuclear deterrence and defense. The lack of a just cause referent inevitably encouraged a quality of abstractness in their analysis. This abstract quality was reinforced by the fact that pronouncements from Rome, whether of the popes or of Vatican II, on issues of war and peace have tended to be very general and clinical, seldom evidencing an awareness that among the "nations" to which they are addressed some are on the side of the Church and its values and some are very definitely not.

Like many official Church pronouncements, including the American Catholic Bishops' 1983 Pastoral Letter, *Gaudium et Spes,* Vatican II's Pastoral Constitution on the Church in the Modern World, moves fitfully and erratically through a maze of complex issues which it often obscures through imprecision.[20] It is worth elaborating on this point since it is clear that *Gaudium et Spes* is the most influential source of official teaching on nuclear deterrence and defense in the Church today and its authority is frequently invoked in the 1983 Pastoral Letter of the American Catholic Bishops.

Gaudium et Spes is often quoted for its judgment that "Any act of war aimed indiscriminately at the destruction of entire cities or of extensive areas along with their population is a crime against God and man himself. It merits unequivocal and unhesitating condemnation."[21] From this condemnation it would be logical to move to a condemnation of the kind of nuclear deterrence that existed in 1965 which was predominantly tending toward so-called countervalue threats to do exactly what the Council condemned and would tend even more in that direction before the counterforce initiatives of the 1970s and 1980s.

The Second Vatican Council, however, did not take this logical step. Instead, it moved on to recognize the modern institution of nuclear deterrence, remarking that "Many regard this state of affairs as the most effective way by which peace of a sort can be maintained between nations at the present time." The Council objected, however, that the "arms race" is "not a safe way to preserve a steady peace" and that the resulting so-called balance of power is no sure path to achieving it.[22]

At the risk of seeming disrespectful, it should be observed that the treatment of deterrence in *Gaudium et Spes* is typical of the fuzzy thinking that has provided the American Catholic Bishops with a superficially impressive backdrop of authority that elicits more respect than it deserves. Typically, the strictures of *Gaudium et Spes* are addressed to "the nations," "the countries," without acknowledgment of the characteristics and relevance to the nuclear deterrence problems of the principal nuclear actors in the international system. Moreover, by failing to sort out the actors in the international system, Vatican II erroneously claims that nuclear deterrence has maintained "some sort of peace," a statement valid only as between the superpowers and their allies, certainly not the hundreds of belligerents in wars fought since 1945. Thus, deterrence is described in a generalized, abstract fashion without reference to actual actors and their rationales in the nuclear deterrent system.

Gaudium et Spes then proceeds, with typical imprecision, to equate "the arms race" with "this form of deterrent." In fact, throughout the document, the terms "arms race" and "deterrence" are used interchangeably.[23] The nuclear deterrence system exists at the moment when adversaries have nuclear weapons with which to threaten each other. The "arms race" is more a buzz word than a term that is defined with any precision when it is denounced by the Church and by peace activists. Any military establishment tries to maintain and improve its capabilities. Whether such natural efforts are always part of an "arms race" and whether arms races are inherently pernicious are controversial issues. They are not resolved by rhetorical flourishes. In any event, one may well have deterrence without an arms race. One may have deterrence while arms control is drastically diminishing nuclear capabilities. Indeed, modern arms control theory and practice emphasizes the absolute necessity of maintaining stable deterrence throughout the arms control process. Arms control experts also warn against destabilizing, dangerous asymmetries resulting from ill-considered arms reductions which leave only one party "racing."[24]

Finally, the proposition that the "arms race," by which is apparently really meant the nuclear deterrence system, is "no infallible way of maintaining real peace" is not new to those who have long wrestled with the practical and moral dilemmas of nuclear deterrence and defense. Of course, nuclear deterrence is no infallible way to real peace. It is the minimal condition for security from nuclear aggression in a world of conflict. Without the "some sort of peace" provided by nuclear deterrence and defense, there is little prospect for "real peace." Once again, the idealist-realist dichotomy is strongly reflected in the differing perspectives and expectations of the authors of *Gaudium et Spes* and those of the Christian realist.[25]

Gaudium et Spes does not provide a good statement of the moral issues of nuclear deterrence. To the best of my knowledge it was not based on even as serious a research and discussion effort as that which contributed to the American Catholic Bishops' 1983 Pastoral Letter. Its handling of the issues is superficial, indeed sloppy. All of this seems to have been obscured, however, by the decision of Vatican II to emphasize escape from the "treacherous trap for humanity" of the balance of terror instead of condemning nuclear deterrence as the logic of its position on countervalue deterrence and war would dictate.[26] In its appeal for a new approach to arms control, based on "an entirely new attitude," Vatican II enjoined an approach to nuclear deterrence and defense that was in part sensible, in part unrealistic, but which avoided a direct confrontation with the issue of threatening to conduct countervalue war, then the basis for nuclear deterrence.[27]

The sensible component in the advice of Vatican II was the realization that it was more important to encourage efforts to decrease the dangers of nuclear war through arms control than to condemn nuclear deterrence and war as immoral, as some wished then and now. The unrealistic element in the advice of Vatican II was the suggestion that the nuclear deterrence system should be viewed as an unfortunate ephemeral phenomenon of the international system and that, in effect, the price for condoning temporarily the continuation of deterrence was the serious arms control effort necessary to eliminate, first, nuclear weapons, then, all international conflict.[28]

It makes sense to say that, because the nuclear balance of terror is precarious, every effort should be made to mitigate its risks by arms control measures. It does not make sense to say that arms control efforts must necessarily succeed in eliminating nuclear deterrence altogether and that such success is the condition for interim toleration of continued nuclear deterrence. If the purposes for nuclear deterrence continue to exist, if the need to deter nuclear aggression in a dangerous world of conflict persists, as seems overwhelmingly likely, then the need for nuclear deterrence will continue even if there is substantial success through arms control in reducing the risks of nuclear war.

One ought not to place a condition—in this case some undefined degree of progress, or at least earnestness on our side, in arms control—on the presently indispensable means of protecting the free world without understanding the necessity of that protection. Since Vatican II eschewed exploration of the threats that occasioned the deterrence system in the first place and that continue to the present, the Council was not in a position to condition nuclear deterrence on anything except compliance with just war requirements. This the Council did not do, any more than the American Catholic Bishops did in 1983. There has never been any interest in developing a morally usable nuclear deterrent in official Church pronouncements, only in eliminating nuclear deterrence, nuclear weapons and war itself, the usual Christian idealist position.[29]

A Christian realist would have wished that Vatican II had seriously considered the continuing threats to the free world and to the Church from Communist powers in the light of the perennial need of free nations for security from aggression. These would have been "signs of the times" as pertinent as some others that were noticed. Had a Christian realist view prevailed at Vatican II, support and guidance would have been provided for those entrusted with the responsibility to provide just and limited deterrence and defense as the basis for free world security and realistic arms control. But Vatican II never reached this degree of seriousness with respect to the dilemmas of nuclear deterrence and defense.

Thus, from *Gaudium et Spes* there developed the concept of deterrence as an abstraction, a necessary evil condoned, that was to be permitted to continue provisionally, subject to the condition that all efforts would be made to eliminate nuclear deterrence through drastic arms control progress. This moral imperative was promulgated to the anonymous nations of the international community without distinction as to their comparative justice as polities or record of threatening or resisting aggression.

Eighteen years later this approach is being put to the test by the American Catholic Bishops. Building on *Gaudium et Spes*, the Bishops have been stressing two themes. One is that the kind of countervalue mutual assured destruction (MAD) deterrence system that has been the basis—at least in declaratory policy—for U.S. and Western strategic nuclear deterrence is immoral on its face. The other is that the continuation of nuclear deterrence in some form can be condoned only in the manner of Vatican II, as a temporary posture strictly conditioned on the pursuit of arms control efforts designed to eliminate nuclear weapons and nuclear deterrence with, in effect, all deliberate speed.

By stressing these two points the American Catholic Bishops have substantially repeated the errors of *Gaudium et Spes*. First, they have concluded, admittedly after much more lengthy consideration than Vatican II, that nuclear deterrence must ultimately lead to levels of nuclear war that by any just war standard are immoral. Second, the Bishops apparently hold, behind their "centimeter of ambiguity," that some kind of abstract deterrence can be condoned pending elimination of nuclear weapons through arms control.

Unlike the statements on nuclear deterrence by modern popes and Vatican II, the pronouncements of the American Catholic Bishops on the subject, from 1968 to the 1983 Pastoral Letter, have been progressively more informed and sophisticated regarding the various strategies and forms of nuclear deterrence and defense. It is not possible to criticize the American Catholic Bishops for condemning nuclear deterrence in sweeping, mono-lithic terms without having explored the possibilities of selective, flexible response deterrence and limited nuclear war. The American Bishops have explored these options to some extent and this constitutes progress.

However, the exploration of nuclear deterrence and war-fighting options short of the clearly suicidal and immoral policies such as MAD suffers from the fundamental flaw of excessive idealism discussed at the outset of this chapter. Since 1968 the American Catholic Bishops have always treated nuclear deterrence as something between a necessary evil and an unnecessary evil, with an increasing propensity toward the latter. They have consistently emphasized the horrors of nuclear war and brushed quickly by the threats to freedom and fundamental human rights that necessitate risking the horrors of nuclear war through maintenance of nuclear deterrence/defense postures. Following the lead of Vatican II, the American Catholic Bishops have treated nuclear deterrence as eminently dispensable rather than indispensable.[30]

In the absence of any serious effort to state the just causes and the threats to them that necessitate nuclear deterrence and defense, as discussed above, the American Catholic Bishops tend to treat nuclear deterrence as a monolithic instrument of defense policy that is both incredibly dangerous and ultimately unnecessary. Since it is viewed far more as an unnecessary than a necessary evil, the burden of proof is placed overwhelmingly on those who would justify continuation of nuclear deterrence in any form. Had the American Catholic Bishops, and the Fathers of Vatican II before them, considered that some kind of nuclear deterrent was a practical and moral necessity to protect the free world from nuclear intimidation and aggression by the Soviet Union and other Communist adversaries pledged to the destruction of everything that the free world and the Church stand for, they would at least have considered the task of finding a morally permissible form of nuclear deterrence to be a necessary one to which they themselves had a responsibility to offer guidance. However, since both the Council Fathers and the American Catholic Bishops take the idealist position that nuclear deterrence and defense are not legitimate necessities but unfortunate evils that are probably unnecessary, they place a moral presumption against nuclear deterrence and defense in any form and throw the burden of overcoming that presumption upon those who claim that just and limited nuclear deterrence and defense are both necessary and feasible.

The position of *Gaudium et Spes* and the 1983 Pastoral Letter is that there is really no great moral dilemma of finding the permissible nuclear means necessary to protect the just causes of the free world. The dilemma is that "the nations" are in a predicament that threatens the physical destruction of the world by nuclear war and that "the nations" must all cooperate to eliminate this threat. The dilemma is not that of finding a just and limited nuclear deterrence/defense posture for the free world. It is the dilemma of dismantling a terribly dangerous and essentially unnecessary balance of terror.

From these perspectives, nuclear deterrence and war have been reduced again to the monolithic, self-evidently immoral, category of earlier Church pronouncements. The possibilities for morally permissible nuclear deterrence and defense have been investigated, found wanting, and rejected. All nuclear deterrence and war is to be judged in terms of the worst case models of nuclear deterrence and war. To be sure, no one can prove or disprove whether nuclear war can be limited and no one is anxious to conduct experiments on this subject. There are a number of technical and human vulnerabilities in any nuclear deterrence/defense system and scenario. Loss of control—through command, control and communication (C^3) and other technical failures, as well as from the inability of human beings to handle a nuclear war environment—is usually foremost in the list of problems confronting efforts to develop limited nuclear deterrence/ defense options. The Bishops choose to believe that nuclear war will inevitably escalate, "escape control," irrespective of the intentions of those who initiate it. It is believed, moreover, that proportionate and discriminate targeting may well be impossible. The argument is shut off with quotations from former high governmental officials and military commanders who admit that they have no confidence in man's ability to limit nuclear war once it has started.[31]

To the Christian realist, these difficulties present agonizing challenges that would be gladly forgone, were some form of nuclear deterrence and defense not a practical and moral necessity. Combining this conviction with commitment to just war standards, the Christian realist, with Father John Courtney Murray, sees a moral imperative to work for the realization of just and limited means of deterrence and defense, both nuclear and conventional.[32]

But what is a necessity, even a moral imperative, to the Christian realist is, for the Christian idealist, a quixotic and dangerous effort to attempt something that is probably impossible, certainly immensely risky, and, most importantly, unnecessary. There is no need, the idealist says, for nuclear deterrence and defense in any form. The task is to eliminate nuclear weapons, not to try to find morally permissible uses for them. So the idealists, and notably the American Catholic Bishops in their 1983 Pastoral Letter, conclude that unless and until it can be proven beyond question that just and limited nuclear deterrence/defense policies are feasible, they must be considered to be impossible. There is, moreover, no disposition to encourage a further search for morally usable nuclear options.[33]

The popes and Vatican II, then, were right in the first place to treat nuclear deterrence and war as an undifferentiated category that, for purposes of moral analyses, should always be viewed in its most absolute, unlimited, unthinkable form. Ironically, this has been the American Catholic Bishops' position even as the United States has moved away significantly from the extreme forms of countervalue, countercity strategic defense postures that characterized earlier policies. This fact is noted by the Bishops but they do not find reassuring the improvements in the direction of emphasis on militargeting in U.S. policies. Rather than encourage further movement in the direction of limited nuclear options, they would counsel all-out arms control initiatives to eliminate nuclear deterrence and weapons entirely.[34]

However, even though they address the threats to the free world only belatedly, reluctantly and with considerable reflection of the view that we are as much if not more to be feared than the Communists, the Bishops do not wholly discount the need for some kind of nuclear deterrent for the immediate future. If any kind of reliance on nuclear weapons is too dangerous to countenance, how can even a temporary deterrent be maintained?

The answer is the bluff deterrent. A bluff deterrent is one in which the party has the capability of carrying out the threat of a nuclear reaction to aggression but does not have the intention and/or will to do so. If it is thought that some kind of nuclear deterrent were temporarily necessary pending arms control breakthroughs that would obviate its necessity, it would be convenient to have the appearance of a deterrent for protection without actually intending to carry out the deterrent threat.[35]

Particularly if it were thought that the most effective deterrence comes from the most immoral, "unthinkable" threats, as in the extreme forms of MAD, it would be conceivable that one could hold out all appearances of being willing to carry out these threats without actually intending to do so. This line of thought is encouraged by the esoteric nominalism of some strategic thinking. The point is constantly made in deterrence theory that the purpose of nuclear weapons deployed in a deterrent posture is that they will never have to be used—if the deterrent works. Drawing on the free-form pop sociology and psychology of some international relations approaches, it is possible to conjure up the proposition that the whole deterrence relationship is infinitely more a matter of "perception" than of substance. It is not what exists that counts, but what the adversary thinks exists.[36]

This kind of approach enhances an unfortunate impression that some seem to draw from the distinction between "deterrence only" and "deterrence plus" strategies. Deterrence only strategies, such as MAD, place such reliance on the deterrent effect of the threat of incredbly horrendous responses to aggression that it is considered to be subversive of the deterrent effect to speculate about the war-fighting strategies that would actually be followed if somehow the deterrent failed. Deterrence plus simply means that it is recognized than any deterrent can fail and if it does it is necessary to have some plans for war-fighting.[37] Somehow the emphases on the psychological, perception aspect of deterrence and the concept of "deterrence only" strategies leads to the notion that one may have nuclear deterrence without the contingency of nuclear war-fighting, something that would be true only if there were an absolute certainty that the deterrent-only deterrent would never fail.

From such concepts developed the bluff deterrent idea articulated in 1976 by Father Bryan Hehir, destined to be the American Catholic Bishops' National Security Adviser. Father Hehir, as a student of *Realpolitik*, recognized the need for a nuclear deterrent. As a moralist he found the MAD deterrent morally untenable. As a student of *Realpolitik* he had, on the one hand, concluded that selective, flexible response limited nuclear deterrence/defense were too problematic and risky to serve as the basis for Western deterrence. On the other hand, he had been duly impressed by the potential of the perceptions emphasis in international relations and deterrence theory and the concept of deterrence only pushed to the extreme meaning of deterrence without war-fighting. From this combination of moral and empirical expertise and insights came the bluff deterrent.[38]

The specific form that the bluff deterrent concept was to take was through the formulation of an issue of "possession" of nuclear weapons. Father Hehir knew, as the Bishops acknowledge in their 1983 Pastoral

Letter, that in order to have a deterrence system you must have the capabilities for assured retaliation against aggression, the intention and will to use those capabilities, and the means to communicate your ability and readiness to carry out your threats to the adversary.[39] In plain language, to have an effective deterrent you have to be able and willing to fight a war if the deterrent threat is defied. But if you bring yourself to believe that the whole business of deterrence is more psychological than substantive, more a matter of perception than of reality, then perhaps you can get away with a bluff deterrent based on one element, capabilities, without the others, intention and will to use the capabilities communicated to the adversary. Great reliance is placed on the ingenious proposition that the adversary will not believe you or trust you to hold to your moral scruples, an interesting reversal of the usual notion of credibility.[40]

Although the concept of bluff deterrence does not long survive serious examination (e.g., how do you simultaneously communicate an intention and will to do something you believe you cannot do morally to your adversary and to your own personnel in the deterrence/defense chain of command?), it recommended itself to Bishops anxious to condemn deterrence generally while condoning it temporarily on condition that arms control progress would be made to eliminate the problem. Hence the usage "possession" of nuclear weapons as something separate from the other components of a nuclear deterrence deployment, e.g., facilities and arrangements to fire the weapons, and the other components of deterrence, e.g., intention, will and their communication to the adversary.

The period 1968–79 saw a succession of statements by the U.S. Catholic Bishops obviously reflecting the bluff deterrent concept. Nuclear deterrence was condemned even more explicitly than it had been in *Gaudium et Spes* but the effect of the condemnations was mitigated by the concession that a kind of deterrence could be maintained based on possession of nuclear weapons until the moment when arms control progress made possible their elimination.[41] Early in the elaborate drafting process of the 1983 Pastoral Letter, the issue of possession of nuclear weapons was still raised. By the time that the final version was voted on by the Bishops in May 1983, the possession issue as such had been removed, perhaps as a result of Christian realist criticism.[42]

Nevertheless, the bluff deterrent lives on in the 1983 Pastoral Letter. If one re-reads the letter often enough, one comes away with the impression that the Bishops intended to admit that some kind of nuclear deterrent must be accepted for the time being. It clearly cannot be anything like a basic MAD countervalue deterrent based on an actual intention to carry out the MAD countervalue threats if the deterrent failed. On the other hand, every effort to develop alternative, counterforce-emphasis limited nuclear deterrence based on just and limited war-fighting strategies is rejected as too risky. The result is a kind of "none of the above" treatment of nuclear options. The Bishops can think of no morally permissible nuclear option. The burden of proof is on those who claim that there might be some. However, the Bishops discourage any attempt to overcome the moral presumption against just and limited nuclear options by trying to develop the capabilities to carry them out.[43]

In these circumstances, of what does the existing nuclear deterrent that is being condoned consist? If no available form of nuclear war-fighting is morally permissible, as the Bishops all but declare, then the bluff deterrent is all that is left. This bluff deterrent is based solely on the possession of nuclear weapons. This possession is accompanied, if we are to take the Bishops seriously, not simply by a negative lack of intention and will to use nuclear weapons against an aggressor but by a positive public commitment never to use nuclear weapons. If this is not a fair reading of the 1983 Pastoral Letter, let the Bishops emerge from behind their centimeter of ambiguity and set the record straight.

The bluff deterrent concept is reinforced in the 1983 Pastoral Letter by enthusiastic espousal of an abstract "deterrence only" position. The Bishops quote the authority of Pope John Paul's view that deterrence can only be condoned, "not as an end in itself but as a step on the way toward progressive disarmament."[44] But deterrence is not an end in itself. It is, first, the indispensable basis for free world security and, second, but only second, the indispensable basis for any lasting arms control progress.

Deterrence is not an abstraction. It is a real world system based on the credible capability, intention and willingness, communicated to an adversary to resist aggression, particularly nuclear aggression, by a defensive nuclear war. It is not an end in itself but a means to an end, just defense. There is, in the real world, no "deterrence only" option in the literal sense that one may have nuclear deterrence without the distinct possibility of having to fight a nuclear war if deterrence fails. The 1983 Pastoral Letter apparently will condone nuclear deterrence that "exists only to prevent the *use* of nuclear weapons." (original emphasis)[45] However, it opposes "planning for prolonged periods of repeated nuclear strikes and counterstrikes, or 'prevailing' in nuclear war," as "not acceptable."[46] The Bishops conclude that such efforts "encourage notions that nuclear war can be engaged in with tolerable human and moral consequences. Rather, we must continually say no to the idea of nuclear war."[47]

If deterrence can fail, and it can, and if a victim of aggression had to choose between surrender and resistance against a nuclear aggressor, is there any alternative to planning and preparing for that dread eventuality and trying to find ways to mitigate its horrors and to terminate it on some basis that would preserve freedom? The question does not arise if one takes an extreme "deterrence only" view and simply refuses to imagine deterrence failing. It does not arise if one is prepared to surrender if the deterrence fails.

There is a third alternative. Perhaps we will be saved the red or dead choice by the overwhelming sweep and pace of arms control agreements which will eliminate nuclear weapons, nuclear deterrence and, ultimately, war itself. A truly Christian idealist solution. But even granting for the sake of argument the remote possibility of some of these achievements, what happens to the nuclear deterrence system while all of these unprecedented breakthroughs are taking place? How many years will it take to obviate the necessity for nuclear deterrence? Will a bluff deterrent hold indefinitely while arms control proceeds? These are questions that the Bishops preferred not to address. They preferred to say no to nuclear war but the Christian realist finds that a simplistic, question-begging, escapist response to the dilemmas of deterrence and defense in an age of conflict wherein the basic freedom and human rights that the Church holds so dear are endangered.

The Christian realist sees a perennial need for armed coercion, within polities and between them. Since nuclear weapons cannot be uninvented, this need will include nuclear coercion. That being the case, the Christian realist sees the problem of nuclear war as one of mitigation and control, not elimination. No arms control "progress" will change this fundamental fact and certainly no reliance on a bluff deterrent that cannot be backed up by effective just and limited defense against aggression will be responsive to the challenges of war.

Whether such a just and limited nuclear deterrence/defense posture is feasible today is very much in question but the prospects are not hopeless.[48] For the Christian realist, the challenge of war is not to eliminate it but to make limited war, the foundation of a morally acceptable deterrent, possible. In a nuclear age this means just and limited nuclear deterrence and defense, the sole realistic basis for the security of the free world and for arms control.

NOTES

1. National Conference of Catholic Bishops, *The Challenge of Peace: God's Promise and Our Response* (Washington, D.C.: United States Catholic Conference, 1983).

2. " 'Only a centimeter of doubt' has prevented the U.S. Catholic Conference of Bishops from declaring their support of an all-out ban on nuclear weapons, Rev. J. Bryan Hehir, director of the Office of International Justice and Peace of the U.S. Catholic Conference, told a meeting of the World Affairs Council in Boston last night." Judy Foreman, " 'Centimeter of Doubt' for Bishops on N-ban," Boston *Globe* (March 1, 1983). Father Hehir used the same expression on the NBC special, "The Bishops and the Bomb," shown on May 15, 1983. In a panel discussion at St. Peter's Church in Washington, D.C. in May 1983, Father

Hehir was reported as saying: "If you ask me does it rule out any use of nuclear weaponry under any circumstances, the Letter never says that. There is a centimeter of ambiguity. And on that centimeter of ambiguity the deterrence . . . " Tom Bethell, "The Bishops' Brain," *The American Spectator* (July 1983), p. 3.

3. For idealists' approaches to international relations, see Kenneth E. Boulding, *Conflict and Defense, A General Theory* (New York: Harper & Row, 1962); Grenville Clark and Louis B. Sohn, *World Peace through World Law* (3rd ed., Cambridge, Mass.: Harvard University Press, 1966); John Herz, *Political Realism and Political Idealism* (Chicago: Chicago University Press, 1953); Louis Henkin, *How Nations Behave* (2nd ed., New York: Council on Foreign Relations/Columbia University Press, 1979).

An extraordinary example of an idealist approach is John XXIII, *Pacem in Terris: Peace on Earth* (Washington, D.C.: NCWC, 1963).

For realist approaches to international relations, see E.H. Carr, *International Relations between the Two World Wars* (London: Macmillan, 1947); Hans A. Morgenthau, *Politics among Nations* (New York: Knopf, 1948); Kenneth W. Thompson, *Political Realism and the Crisis of World Politics* (Princeton, N.J.: Princeton University Press, 1960); Reinhold Niebuhr, *Christianity and Power Politics* (New York: Charles Scribner's Sons, 1940); William V. O'Brien, *War and/or Survival* (Garden City, N.Y.: Doubleday, 1969).

A classic critique of idealism and realism is Inis Claude, Jr., *Power and International Relations* (New York: Random House, 1962).

4. See Robert W. Tucker, *The Just War* (Baltimore, Md.: The Johns Hopkins University Press, 1960).

5. See James E. Dougherty and Robert L. Pfaltzgraf, Jr., *Contending Theories of International Relations* (Philadelphia: J.B. Lippincott, 1971), Chapter 7, pp. 251–300; on psychological factors in deterrence, pp. 375–78.

6. On just war doctrine, see John Courtney Murray, S.J., *We Hold These Truths* (New York: Sheed & Ward, 1960), Chapters 10 and 11, pp. 221–72; Paul Ramsey, *The Just War: Force and Political Responsibility* (New York: Charles Scribner's Sons, 1968); James T. Johnson, *Ideology, Reason and Limitation of War* (Princeton, N.J.: Princeton University Press, 1975) and *Just War Tradition and the Restraint of War* (Princeton, N.J.: Princeton University Press, 1981); William V. O'Brien, *The Conduct of Just and Limited War* (New York: Praeger, 1981); David Hollenbach, S.J., *Nuclear Ethics* (New York: Paulist Press, 1983).

For a thorough and fair compendium and analysis of American Catholic writing on nuclear war and morality, see Judith A. Dwyer, S.S.J., "An Analysis of Nuclear Warfare in Light of the Traditional Just War Theory: An American Roman Catholic Perspective (1945–1981)." (Ph.D. dissertation, The Catholic University of America, 1983.)

7. See O'Brien, *Conduct of Just and Limited War,* Chapter 2, pp. 13–38.

8. *Ibid.,* pp. 35–36; William V. O'Brien, "Just-War Doctrine in a Nuclear Context," *Theological Studies* 44 (June 1983), p. 197.

9. NCCB, *Challenge of Peace*, I, C3, 80–110.

10. *Ibid.*, II, 122.

11. O'Brien, *War and/or Survival*, pp. 112–14.

12. NCCB, *Challenge of Peace*, II, D2, 167–99.
13. *Ibid.*, III, B2, 245–50.
14. *Origins* 13 (May 19, 1983). NCCB, *Challenge of Peace*, III, B2, 249.
15. NCCB, *Challenge of Peace*, B2, 250.
16. *Ibid.*, 251.
17. *Ibid.*
18. *Ibid.,* Introduction, 1–4; I, 5; II, A, 130.
19. See the critical view of the Bishops' emphasis on the most catastrophic scenarios for nuclear war and their down-grading of the consequences of failure to protect free world security in Albert Wohlstetter, "Bishops, Statesmen, and Other Strategists on the Bombing of Innocents," *Commentary* 75 (June 1983), pp. 15–35.
20. Vatican II, *Pastoral Constitution on the Church in the Modern World (Gaudium et Spes)*, Walter 'M. Abbott, S.J., *The Documents of Vatican II* (New York: Guild/ America/Association, 1966), pp. 199–308.
21. *Ibid.*, no. 80, p. 294.
22. *Ibid.,* no. 81, pp. 294–95.
23. *Ibid.*, nos. 80–82, pp. 293–97.
24. On deterrence, see generally Roger D. Speed, *Strategic Deterrence in the 1980s* (Stanford, Calif.: Hoover Institute, 1979); Patrick M. Morgan, *Deterrence: A Conceptual Analysis* (Beverly Hills, Calif.: Sage, 1977); Donald M. Snow, *Nuclear Deterrence in a Dynamic World* (University, Ala.: University of Alabama Press, 1981); Dougherty and Pfaltzgraf, *Contending Theories of International Relations*, Chapter 9, pp. 368–416.
25. See O'Brien, *War and/or Survival*, pp. 1–68, 112–14.
26. *Gaudium et Spes*, no. 81, p. 295.
27. "All these considerations compel us to undertake an evaluation of war with an entirely new attitude." *Ibid.,* no. 80, p. 293.
28. *Ibid.*, no. 82, pp. 295–97.
29. *Ibid.*
30. See *Human Life in Our Day*, Pastoral Letter of the American Hierarchy, November 15, 1968, *Pastoral Letters of the American Hierarchy, 1792–1970*, nos. 93–132, pp. 694–701; *To Live in Christ Jesus*, A Pastoral Reflection on the Moral Life, November 11, 1976 (Washington, D.C.: United States Catholic Conference, 1976), pp. 30–39; *The Gospel of Peace and the Danger of War*, Statement, USCC Administrative Board, February 15, 1978 (Washington, D.C.: United States Catholic Conference, 1978); Testimony of John Cardinal Krol, representing the U.S. Catholic Conference before the Senate Foreign Relations Committee, September 6, 1979, in *The Nuclear Threat: Reading the Signs of the Times*, Patricia L. Rengel, ed. (Washington, D.C.: Office of International Justice and Peace/USCC, October 1979).
31. It should be observed that the definition of the war-conduct principles of proportion and discrimination is scarcely a matter for debate in *The Challenge of Peace*, since it is assumed that nuclear war will almost certainly escalate and/or escape control to a point where it is disproportionate and indiscriminate by any standard.

See NCCB, *Challenge of Peace,* II, C, 144–45, 152–53; D, 179–80.

32. See Murray, *We Hold These Truths*, pp. 270–71.

33. NCCB, *Challenge of Peace*, II, D2, 178–99.

34. *Ibid.*

35. On bluff deterrents, see Ramsey, *Just War*, pp. 249–58 and his disavowal of the idea in Paul Ramsey, "A Political Ethics Context for Strategic Thinking," in Morton A. Kaplan, ed., *Strategic Thinking and its Moral Implications* (Chicago: University of Chicago Center for Policy Study, 1973), p. 142.

The central source of the Bishops' bluff deterrent position appears to be Father Hehir's parts of Robert A. Gessert and J. Bryan Hehir, *The New Nuclear Debate* (New York: Council on Religion and International Affairs, 1976), pp. 44, 47–53, 66–69.

For critical reactions to the bluff deterrent concept, see Wohlstetter, "Bishops, Statesmen, and Other Strategists on the Bombing of Innocents," pp. 16, 30–31; O'Brien, "Just-War Doctrine in a Nuclear Context," pp. 214–16.

36. See, generally, Wohlstetter, "Bishops, Statesmen, and Other Strategists on the Bombing of Innocents." A useful survey is Robert Jervis, "Deterrence Theory Revisited," *World Politics* 31 (January 1979), pp. 289–324.

37. On the "deterrence only"-"deterrence plus" dichotomy, see Wohlstetter's authoritative critique in "Bishops, Statesmen, and Other Strategists on the Bombing of Innocents," especially pp. 30–35. See, generally, Snow, *Nuclear Deterrence in a Dynamic World*, pp. 5–6, 44, 69–73, 79.

See the treatment of deterrence, with emphasis on discouraging deterrence plus planning and policies, NCCB, *Challenge of Peace*, II, D2, 178–99.

38. See Hehir in Gessert and Hehir, *New Nuclear Debate*, pp. 44, 47–53, 66–9.

39. NCCB, *Challenge of Peace*, II, D1, 162–66.

40. See Hehir in Gessert and Hehir, *New Nuclear Debate*, pp. 44, 47–53, 66–9.

41. See the treatment of the issue of possession of nuclear weapons as a discrete subject in *Human Life in Our Day* (1968), no. 106, p. 697, wherein *Gaudium et Spes*, no. 81 is cited as authority for the distinction.

In his testimony before the Senate Foreign Relations Committee Cardinal Krol stated:

The moral judgment of this statement ["To Live in Christ Jesus," 1976] is that not only the *use* of strategic nuclear weapons, but also the *declared intent* to use them involved in our deterrence policy is wrong. This explains the Catholic dissatisfaction with nuclear deterrence and the urgency of the Catholic demand that the nuclear arms race be reversed. It is of the utmost importance that negotiations proceed to meaningful and continuing reductions in nuclear stockpiles, and eventually, to the phasing out altogether of nuclear deterrence and the threat of mutual-assured destruction.

As long as there is hope of this occurring, Catholic moral teaching is willing, while negotiations proceed, to tolerate the possession of nuclear weapons for deterrence as the lesser of two evils. If that hope were to disappear, the moral attitude of the Catholic Church would almost certainly have to shift to one of uncompromising condemnation of both use *and* possession of such weapons. [original emphasis]

The Nuclear Threat, p. 10.

42. In the First Draft Pastoral Letter on Peace and War, then entitled *God's Hope in a Time of Fear*, June 11, 1982, the issue is raised: "If we were to reject any conceivable use of nuclear weapons, we would face the very difficult question *whether it is permissible even to continue to possess nuclear weapons.*" (Working Text, p. 31) [original emphasis]

In the Second Draft Proposed Pastoral Letter, *The Challenge of Peace: God's Promise and Our Response*, General Meeting, November 15–18, 1982, it is contended that "The moral questions about deterrence focus on five issues: (1) the *possession* of weapons of mass destruction. . . . " (Working Text, p. 50) [original emphasis]

In the Third Draft of the Pastoral Letter, May 1983, the discrete issue of possession of nuclear weapons is no longer raised. Instead, emphasis is placed on the necessity that violation of the principles of noncombatant immunity and proportionality not be intended in a strategy of deterrence and that "Deterrence is not an adequate strategy as a long-term basis for peace; it is a transitional strategy justifiable only in conjunction with resolute determination to pursue arms control and disarmament." (Working Text, p. v) The four key issues listed for discussion on p. 66 of the working text do not include possession of nuclear weapons.

The 1983 Pastoral Letter does not distinguish possession of nuclear weapons as a separate subject. It is instructive to observe that quotations from Cardinal Krol's 1979 Senate Foreign Relations Committee statement do not include his separate observations on possession, cited *supra*, note 41. See NCCB, *Challenge of Peace*, II, D2, 170.

43. *Ibid.*, II, C, 157–61; D, 178–99.

44. John Paul II, Message, UN Special Session, 1982, cited in NCCB, *Challenge of Peace*, II, D2, 173.

45. *Ibid.*, 188.

46. *Ibid.*

47. *Ibid.*

48. I survey the problem of just and limited deterrence and defense in *Conduct of Just and Limited War*, pp. 127–44; "Just-War Doctrine in a Nuclear Context," pp. 214–20.

MICHAEL NOVAK

The U.S. Bishops,
The U.S. Government—
and Reality

Michael Novak is Resident Scholar in Religion and Public Policy at the American Enterprise Institute and the author of *Moral Clarity in the Nuclear Age*, *Confession of a Catholic* and *The Spirit of Democratic Capitalism*.

One must not give the impression that the Church does not take sufficiently into account the magnitude of the problems and the seriousness of the tremendous responsibilities of government authorities who have to make decisions in these matters. This does not mean that the Church cannot and must not clearly enunciate the certain and seriously obligatory moral principles that the authorities themselves must keep in mind and follow. This must be done, however, in such a manner that it helps those authorities to get a correct orientation according to the basic principles of human and Christian morals and not to create even greater difficulties for them in an area so enormously difficult and so full of responsibility. The same observations apply also to public opinion.

Cardinal Casaroli to the U.S. Bishops,
Memorandum of meeting Jan. 18–19, 1983[1]

It was inevitable that a statement produced by the U.S. Bishops on nuclear arms during 1982–83 would be interpreted by the press and by governments around the world in political terms. Large and emotional public demonstrations on the subject characterized those two years. The nuclear freeze was a major issue during the U.S. congressional elections of 1982 and during the West German and United Kingdom parliamentary elections of 1983. A crucial vote on the nuclear freeze was scheduled in the U.S. Congress just days from the public release of the second draft of the U.S. Bishops' statement in 1982. On the television news and in the newsmagazines, the subject was inescapable. Moreover, Bishop Leroy Matthiesen of Amarillo, Texas, was featured on the cover of *Life* Magazine, and told *Life* of his zest for "confrontation" between the U.S. Bishops and the U.S. government.[2] Archbishop Raymond Hunthausen of Seattle had won national headlines through urging Catholics to violate the Internal Revenue Service law by withholding the fifty percent of their taxes which, he said (erroneously; the true sum is less than one percent), was being used for nuclear arms.[3]

Meanwhile, the Reagan administration had come under sudden fire from Democrats on the issue of arms control. Because of agreements to meet the threat of the Soviet SS-20s, reached by President Jimmy Carter at the behest of Chancellor Helmut Schmidt of West Germany in 1979, the theater nuclear arms balance in Europe was being decided during 1983. Simultaneously, the Soviet Union had carefully laid out a Western disarmament campaign under the title "The Right to Life," as if stolen directly from the U.S. Bishops.[4] Prudence is a matter of doing the right thing in the right way *at the right time*. In this case the timing of the Bishops' Pastoral gave it unusual political significance, nationally and internationally.

Furthermore, the issues actually addressed by the U.S. Bishops—particularly those concerning the nature of deterrence—were not fundamentally different from those that had obtained thirty years earlier. One might reasonably ask either why the long delay or why the sudden haste? There was no inherent need to rush to judgment, unless, of course, it was the purpose of the Bishops precisely to have political effect, during an unusually sensitive period.

Finally, the Bishops' Pastoral affected a sharp political debate already being conducted within American intellectual life. According to Norman Podhoretz, the author of *The Present Danger* and the editor of *Commentary* magazine, the Pastoral Letter of the U.S. Bishops is "intellectually and morally disgraceful."[5] It is, says Albert Wohlstetter, designed "to give casuistry a bad name."[6] By contrast, McGeorge Bundy, writing in *The New York Review of Books,* praised the Pastoral Letter.[7] Insofar as *Commentary* and *The New York Review of Books* represent two different poles of intellectual debate in the United States, the Catholic Bishops, in tilting toward one side, made a choice.

History alone will show whether what the Bishops declared is an act of moral illumination, as some judge, or rather of moral obscurantism and appeasement, as others judge. Bishops in the past have erred. It cannot be said with certainty that, in this case, they have not. Yet it does seem clear that fifteen years ago no such document as the present one could have been issued. Speaking of the difference in episcopal generations, symbolized at present by Archbishop Philip Hannan and Bishop Thomas Gumbleton, one younger bishop told the *National Catholic Reporter* that "In the fifties, we were all Hannans. Now we're anti-Hannan and pro-Gumbleton."[8] Many would like to think that a superior understanding of the Gospels made the difference. A reading of the text does not establish that. For even at those places where the new text seems to rest on *theological* premises—with references to the theology of peace, to prophecy, to "signs of the times," and "the new moment"—mainly what one sees, instead, is a vision of "progressive" history shared in common by the atheist left and the Bishops. The practical conclusions of the letter offer little comfort to the left, but the *spirit* of the letter the left properly recognizes as its own.

Apart from the geopolitical context and apart from the context of partisan politics, there is also an intramural and ecclesiastical context for this letter. Considering the extreme positions taken by Bishop Gumbleton and Pax Christi, to which some fourscore Bishops subscribe, and the adversarial rhetoric of Bishop Matthiesen, Archbishop Hunthausen, Bishop Sullivan, and others—rhetoric acutely embarrassing to some of their fellow Bishops—it is something of a marvel that the final product (unlike the two earlier drafts) is as good as it is. In this context, I have described it as a "valiant document" and given public thanks for it in the *National Review*.[9]

The prudent intervention of the Vatican on January 18–19, 1983, summarized in nine succinct points by Cardinal Casaroli, has been entirely incorporated into the third draft.[10]

The Bishops have said that the primary purpose of their Pastoral is religious, not political. This may be so. Whatever their intentions, however, the public is correct to discern that the Pastoral's main thrust—at least, as a public fact presented by the media—is political. Whatever the Bishops intended, the Pastoral came to public notice not because of its religious significance but because of its political significance. This was, mainly, what was massively reported around the world. This was what those who are not religious (or, in any case, not Catholic) were mostly concerned about. *What political difference* did the Pastoral make? Let me repeat again: This may not be what the Bishops see in the Letter or what they intended. It is, however, a fact with which political and theological analysts must deal.

The long-term political consequences of the Bishops' Pastoral will not be known for a decade or more. It would be foolish to try to outguess history. But it is not foolish to recognize that such final judgment will depend disproportionately on the deeds of the Soviets. For one major vision of the period 1980–89 is that it is a moment of clear and present danger for the United States, a period during which the correlation of forces between the Soviet Union and the United States is temporarily in favor of the Soviet Union to a degree never reached before nor likely to be reached again, once America has rearmed itself.

According to a second major view, this fear is overwrought. The danger of the present is not the relative military weakness of the United States. The chief danger lies, rather, in a "renewed arms race." By their words and actions, the Bishops have taken the second view. Like Jimmy Carter before the invasion of Afghanistan, the Bishops are exceedingly vulnerable to outbreaks of Soviet aggression, particularly of limited nuclear aggression. Renewed Soviet aggression will win for the Bishops a reputation for misjudgment and appeasement.

Aleksandr Solzhenitsyn, by contrast, has chosen a different form of prophecy. He writes:

> At one time there was no comparison between the strength of the USSR and your own. Then it became equal to yours. Now, as all recognize, it is becoming superior to yours. Perhaps today the ratio is just greater than equal, but soon it will be 2 to 1. Then 3 to 1. Finally it will be 5 to 1. . . . With such nuclear superiority it will be possible to block the use of your weapons, and on some unlucky morning they will declare: "Attention. We're sending our troops into Europe, and if you make a move, we will annihilate you." And this ratio of 3 to 1 or 5 to 1 will have its effect: you will not make a move.[11]

Unlike Solzhenitsyn, the U.S. Bishops do not urge the West to rearm itself to meet the present danger. They throw their weight, instead, on the side of those who counsel disarmament. At a moment of maximum danger, they counselled the ways of good will, negotiations, and trust. What if they were wrong?

The Bishops have, therefore, exercised their right to political judgment. They have committed themselves to a line of thought and action which some applaud and others find terribly mistaken. Moreover, despite the claims of some, the Bishops did not act "courageously." In the political culture of the media, views such as they put forward are routinely praised, as the Bishops were in fact praised. It is those who take the harder line, asking greater discipline, higher defense spending, and a more resolute will, who are most liable to be vilified. The words of Archbishop Hunthausen and Bishops Matthiesen and Gumbleton are avidly reported in the media, while Archbishop Hannan is rendered as a pathetic villain. Taking Hannan's position would have required the strength of prophecy, in the teeth of furious insult from the major media and the Catholic left. As distinct from the 1950s, most of the institutional power of the American Catholic Church is on the left; most magazines, most publishing houses, most figures in authority. Further, the left has popularity in the media denied to the right.

Looking at matters coldly, however, it does not appear that the nuclear policies of the Catholic Bishops actually differ very much from those of successive U.S. governments.

The U.S. Bishops and the U.S. Government

Some Bishops have pictured the Pastoral Letter as a confrontation with the Reagan administration.[12] If this were true of fundamentals, the Bishops would be opposed to the policies of every American administration since World War II, and probably also to the policies of the next administration, even if it is Democratic. In actual fact, however, one must read the Pastoral with a fine mesh to find points of policy or principle on which the Bishops take a position clearly adversarial to those of the U.S. government.

Some will say that the proposal to "halt" rather than to "curb" the development of nuclear weapons[13] illustrates opposition to the Reagan administration. In a minor sense, it does. But when one recalls that the proposed "halt" requires Soviet action, too—it must be "mutual" and "verifiable"—supporting a "halt" is like supporting motherhood and apple pie. It is a way of avoiding (for a time) the actual realities of Soviet power, proclivities, and actions. It merely postpones encounters with reality.

A second purported example concerns "no first use." After a long bit of casuistry on the subject, the Bishops write:

We express repeatedly in this letter our extreme skepticism about the prospects for controlling a nuclear exchange, however limited the first use might be. Precisely because of this skepticism, we judge resort to nuclear weapons to counter a conventional attack to be morally unjustifiable.[14]

At the same time, the Bishops recognize that the correlation of conventional forces on the Western European front may so favor the Soviet Union at present that deterrence of a Soviet conventional attack by a conventional defense may not be possible. They then conclude this section:

We urge NATO to move rapidly toward the adoption of a "no first use" policy, but doing so in tandem with development of an adequate alternative defense posture.[15]

This is exactly the view being urged upon NATO by General Rogers, NATO Supreme Commander. The difficulty is, of course, the reluctance of NATO-member political constituencies to spend more money, raise military conscription efforts, further militarize their societies, and otherwise maintain for years on end the requisite impregnable deterrent force with purely conventional weaponry. A massive political campaign will be necessary to stimulate the political will of democratic peoples. The European peace movement will have to be opposed. Bitter anti-American propaganda will have to be countered. (Soviet propaganda no longer boasts of the glories of the Soviet system; it has switched its international focus to incessant anti-Americanism.) Will the U.S. Bishops have the moral courage to take the lead in these important struggles?

A third purported example is the position of the Bishops on counterforce targeting. The Bishops write:

But "counterforce targeting," while preferable from the perspective of protecting civilians, is often joined with a declaratory policy which conveys the notion that nuclear war is subject to precise rational and moral limits. We have already expressed our severe doubts about such a concept. Furthermore, a purely counterforce strategy may seem to threaten the viability of other nations' retaliatory forces, making deterrence unstable in a crisis and war more likely.[16]

But this judgment, too, is widely shared. The number one moral imperative behind current U.S. policy is to deter any unjust use of nuclear weapons whatever. Targeting civilian populations violates the principle of discrimination. Targeting the nuclear retaliatory weapons of the enemy is morally preferable from that perspective, but involves dangers of its own.

Counterforce targeting is not necessarily joined to the declaratory policy mentioned by the Bishops, however; it is probably the most effective dissuader for the Soviets, whose power rests on weapons, not consent. A real capacity to destroy the enemy's retaliatory force gives that enemy pause. Some in the U.S. have become alarmed at the Soviet capacity to destroy nearly all U.S. land-based missiles and bomber fleets even though the sixteen U.S. submarines usually on station still seem safe. The submarines are least adequate for counterforce targeting.

But here, too, the Bishops reach the same position as the U.S. government. They write:

> Although reasons exist which move some to condemn reliance on nuclear weapons for deterrence, we have not reached this conclusion for the reasons outlined in this letter.[17]

Even when we look at the three specific proposals which the Bishops oppose and the six which they recommend, differences with U.S. government policy are minimal. One does best to read these proposals with actual Soviet capacities in mind. Thus, the Bishops oppose:

> 1. The addition of weapons which are likely to be vulnerable to attack, yet also possess a "prompt hard-target kill" capability that threatens to make the other side's retaliatory forces vulnerable. Such weapons may seem to be useful primarily in a first strike; we resist such weapons for this reason and we oppose Soviet deployment of such weapons which generate fear of a first strike against U.S. forces.
> 2. The willingness to foster strategic planning which seeks a nuclear war-fighting capacity that goes beyond the limited function of deterrence outlined in this letter.
> 3. Proposals which have the effect of lowering the nuclear threshold and blurring the difference between nuclear and conventional weapons.[18]

One can easily understand these moral scruples of the Bishops. But their opposition on these three points would make more sense if the Soviets were different from what they have shown themselves to be. The Soviets *have* deployed "prompt hard-target kill" weapons. The Soviets *do* have "first strike" weapons deployed, in redundant numbers. The Soviet *do* foster strategic planning—and tactical planning—for nuclear war-fighting. And, finally, the Soviets *do* blur the difference between nuclear and conventional weapons, both in theoretical writings and in the spectrum of weapons actually deployed.

The moral question which the Bishops evade by simply "opposing" such proposals—for the Soviets, these have moved beyond the stage of "proposals" and have long been realities—is what the United States ought to do, to deter unjust use by the USSR of such formidable assets. The Bishops simply say they "oppose" U.S. proposals to meet assets with assets. But just how, then, will the Soviets be deterred? It is not moral to allow a nation, particularly a nation like the USSR, to possess such assets undeterred. It is a moral obligation to find suitable instruments for such deterrence.

Obviously, moralists prefer clarity. They would not like distinctions "blurred" (objection 3); nor contingency strategic planning in case, however remotely, an actual nuclear exchange happens to be limited (objection 2); nor an American first-strike capacity to match what the Soviets now have (objection 1). But often reality is not as clear as moralists would like it to be. Concrete judgment is needed. That is why the individual confessor in the confessional must apply moral principles to a concrete human being, and why individual public officials must apply moral principles to intractable realities. It would certainly be a morally better world if the USSR did *not* have a first-strike capacity, *nor* engage in strategic planning for nuclear war-fighting, nor blur differences between conventional and nuclear forces. But such a world no longer exists.

Exactly here is where the U.S. government needs moral guidance, and yet none is offered. What should the U.S. government do? The Bishops propose that "sufficiency" to deter is an adequate strategy; the quest for nuclear superiority must be rejected. But if U.S. land-based retaliatory forces are vulnerable to a Soviet first-strike capability, what does "sufficiency" demand? If the USSR makes plans for limited nuclear exchanges, what does "sufficiency" demand? The Bishops here evade answers which the U.S. commander-in-chief morally cannot evade.

In support of the concept of "sufficiency," the Bishops make six recommendations, five of which are of a wishful sort. The first is the nuclear "halt" described above. The second is for negotiated bilateral deep cuts in the nuclear arsenals of both sides, as proposed by the U.S. in Geneva. The third is for "early and successful conclusion of negotiations of a comprehensive test ban treaty." The fourth is "removal by all parties of short-range nuclear weapons." The fifth is "removal by all parties of nuclear weapons from areas where they are likely to be overrun in the early stages of war." The sixth recommendation requires greater expenditures on nuclear forces and is already underway in the U.S.: "Strengthening of command and control over nuclear weapons."

The first three of these recommendations place great faith in negotiations; to them we shall return. As for number four, just *how* will the Bishops oblige the Soviets to remove their short-range nuclear weapons from the Western front? The fifth point affects only the U.S., since NATO forces cannot possibly overrun Warsaw Pact forces, not being equipped for offensive attack. Only the Soviets threaten to overrun European territory.

Perhaps we can conclude this section summarily. There are few if any ways in which the Bishops actually diverge from the policy of the U.S. government. The moral questions they raise have often been raised before, while their systematic presentation in one place heightens our sense of complexity. On the other side of the ledger, the tidiness of such systematic thinking can only seem enviable, given "the magnitude of the problems and the seriousness of the tremendous responsibilities of government authorities who have to make decisions in these matters," as Cardinal Casaroli wisely put it.

Just and Unjust Negotiations

The Bishops place great faith, as we have seen, in negotiations. Indeed, the three recommendations mentioned a moment ago derive from the Bishops' general principle: "Nuclear deterrence should be used as a step on the way toward progressive disarmament." "Progressive" sounds odd here. Can the Bishops possibly mean "progressive" in the generic sense of "socialist"? They cannot mean *unilateral* disarmament, which they say they are against. So they must mean "negotiated" disarmament. But far from being "progressive," disarmament efforts during the last century or so are extremely disheartening. Consider the judgment cited by Barbara Tuchman:

> The trouble with disarmament was (and still is) that the problem of war is tackled upside down and at the wrong end. . . . Nations don't distrust each other because they are armed; they are armed because they distrust each other. And therefore to want disarmament before a minimum of common agreement on fundamentals is as absurd as to want people to go undressed in winter.[19]

Even Theodore Draper, writing in *The New York Review of Books*, is not very encouraging.

> Once different weapons and even different weapons systems must be evaluated and balanced off against each other, negotiations inevitably degenerate into endlessly futile haggling sessions, brought to a close only by agreement on a crazy quilt of trade-offs and loopholes. Negotiations of this sort become more important for the mere consolation that the deadly antagonists are negotiating than for anything the negotiations may bring forth. . . . Short of abolishing all

nuclear weapons forever and everywhere, deterrence is all we have.[20]

Has disarmament been "progressive" since the Napoleonic wars? Since the Civil War, or 1914, or 1945? Has the Soviet Union ever disarmed in any respect whatever?[21] After 1968, Defense Secretary McNamara expected that a virtual U.S. nuclear freeze would enable the Soviets to come up to parity and halt. They did not.

Indeed, two major examples of "progressive disarmament" that historians can point to—apart from the enforced disarming of West Germany and Japan following World War II—have been conducted by the U.S. The first was the demobilization of U.S. forces in Europe within eighteen months of the cessation of hostilities, which F.D. Roosevelt rashly promised the unbelieving Stalin at Yalta. The second was the *relative* nuclear disarmament of the U.S. since 1968, under the McNamara illusion of Soviet imitation. Congress after Congress was elected in the 1970s to "cut the defense budget." Indeed, the U.S. budget for defense went *down* by 19 percent in constant 1983 dollars from 1970 until 1981—from $223 billion to $182 billion.[22] Moreover, since 1968, the number of land-based missile launchers has remained constant at 1054. The number of strategic bombers has fallen by attrition from 1364 in 1964 to 272 in 1983. The nuclear warheads in its arsenal have been reduced in number and size. The total throwweight of all its nuclear warheads has been reduced by more than half.[23]

Oddly, the Bishops do not *praise* the United States for such "progressive disarmament." To do so would call attention to the feverish and herculean efforts of the USSR to achieve something far beyond nuclear parity (which was publicly declared to exist in 1972): both nuclear and conventional superiority in every field. Here, the Bishops enter the field of moral wistfulness. They write: "We must continually say no to the idea of nuclear war." Such words are not like the words of transubstantiation; saying no does not change reality. Nor will "progressive disarmament" occur because the Bishops need it in order to justify, by their lights, moral reliance on deterrence. Deterrence is morally obligatory *whether or not* "progressive disarmament" leaps from the world of myth into the world of fact. It will be even more necessary if it does not.

For the Bishops assume that the Soviets *will* disarmament. This is a fundamental misunderstanding. Neither the Marxist ideology about the moral *obligation* to use force in history nor the practice of the Soviets since 1917 gives any empirical support to such an assumption. When the U.S. reduced its nuclear forces, the USSR could have caught up and rested; it did not. We must assume that the USSR does what it wills to do. The USSR wills to negotiate nothing except the permanent inferiority of the United

States, and a consequent pattern of subservience to the "laws of history." This cannot be negotiated in justice.

The world has long had a moral theory about justice in war. A classical statement of moral guidance for justice in negotiations does not yet exist. For it cannot be asserted that all negotiations are morally just. Some negotiations succeed through intimidation; some through cowardice. The ill and dying Roosevelt at Yalta was rude toward Churchill, fawning toward Stalin, and catastrophically unjust to the peoples of Eastern Europe.[24] These same peoples had already suffered more than their share through earlier unjust negotiations, the Molotov-Ribbentrop Pact. Some believe the Helsinki Accords added to the injustice, in as yet unmeasured ways. Whatever the moral status of particular cases, it seems obvious that negotiations between great powers cannot escape moral scrutiny. The Catholic Bishops have given thought to the morality of warfare, but very little to the calculus of moral evils involved inevitably in every negotiation aimed at peace.

Two more examples bear on the point. The "unconditional surrender" imposed by the allies on Germany after World War II was not clearly an act of moral justice. Neither were the negotiations at Versailles at the end of World War I.

In all negotiations, the weaker party may be obliged to accept injustice. One cannot, therefore, as the Bishops do, simply judge deterrence by the outcome of negotiations. One must, rather, judge the outcome of negotiations by the power of deterrence. Factors of power are of elementary importance.

Further, the asymmetry between democratic states and totalitarian states *ipso facto* injures the moral standing of negotiations. Democratic peoples reach consensus through public contests, and therefore typically negotiate first against themselves; totalitarian powers wait and watch. (They also penetrate domestic debates within open societies.)

Power in totalitarian states rests in the will of a collective few, insulated from public discussion, operating in secrecy, and bound to no moral law but their own aggrandizement. In democratic states, one government is not always like another; public consensus shifts; moral standards and public laws have enormous public power even in compelling presidential resignations. It is difficult, therefore, to imagine wholly moral and just relations between democratic and totalitarian states. Agreements between them can only be codified statements of existing correlations of force and national interest.

Finally, as between democratic and totalitarian powers, the aim of negotiations, once entered into, is quite different. Totalitarian states have no need to reach an agreement. They can be sublimely indifferent. They can concentrate every energy upon one sole aim: increasing their power by every possible degree. For their legitimacy does not flow from the esteem of others but from their own tightly clenched power. By contrast, once negotiations are entered into by democratic powers, democratic leaders are quickly blamed according to standards of universal reason and moral principle. To come home with "nothing" is for them, but not for totalitarian leaders, a public failure. Consequently, it is relatively easy for totalitarian masters of the dynamics of negotiations to concentrate attention upon cosmetic concessions, amounting to words meaningful only within free, open and moral societies and having no substance whatever within regimes based upon lies. Furthermore, Western negotiators typically want agreements that are simple, clear, and easy to "verify." They define weapons systems and other military matters in this light, which is often a false light.[25]

In a word, negotiating with a totalitarian power like the Soviet Union can never be like negotiating with partners who share a similar moral vision, intellectual tradition, or common meanings to undergird bare words on documents. The language of such negotiations is, inevitably, like Alice in Wonderland. Typically, too, serious issues are relegated to unsigned appendices and memoranda of understanding, with a proviso that all parties understand them according to their own laws, institutions, customs, and authorities.

From these plain facts, there is a strong case to be made that *any* negotiation with a totalitarian power is *inherently* unjust and, if just, only so by accident, as it suits the totalitarian power. Parchment barriers do not bind those whose power comes from no parchment. "Justice" can have no meaning to a party not bound to it.

"Progressive disarmament" is, therefore, a wish, a touching plea. It is a phrase uttered by those who despair of the real-world competition of military power. Giving up *that* struggle, they plead with the stronger power to do likewise. Whatever else it is, this plea is not Christian morality, only a Nietzschean parody thereof.

While negotiations with the Soviets must, for various reasons, go on, they can only be as effective as the military power which bends Soviet will. What Soviet morality compels Soviet will to desire in the absence of constraining force is shown in sixty-six years of bloody history. Since 1923, Soviet authorities have put 65 million of their own citizens to death for political reasons; they have also subjugated some 31 nations.[26]

Indeed, one has only to alter the subject of "progressive disarmament" from "Soviets" to "Nazis" to see the absurdity of identifying religious hope with confidence in the reasonable mercies of totalitarian leaders.

Two Scenarios

Throughout their letter, the Bishops seem to assume that the threat of nuclear war emanates most from American actions; their arguments are couched for American ears. Yet suppose that the United States were unilaterally to disarm. Nuclear arsenals in the hands of Soviet leaders—and in those of several weaker powers, including China—would then even more dramatically pose the threat of nuclear war. For the single greatest threat of nuclear war emanates from the Soviet Union. The Soviet Union has a doctrine which imposes on its loyal believers an obligation to make socialism triumph universally. This doctrine holds to such triumph through force. Secondly, the succession of leadership in the USSR is still unsettled; the military, KGB, and the Party compete under fragile rules. Thirdly, Russian traditions of imperial prerogative have a certain weight. Military superiority is important to the Soviet state as to no other, for no other has so ample a sense of destiny. From the Soviet viewpoint, socialism is the tide of history, the Soviet state its vanguard, the Red Army its sword.

Furthermore, during the past ten years three fundamental changes have occurred in the correlation of forces between the USSR and the United States, which seem to confirm the Soviet vision of history. (1) After the Cuban missile crisis, Soviet *strategic* nuclear forces made such dramatic leaps forward that they were announced to be at "rough parity" to American strategic forces by the time of the SALT I agreements of 1972; since then, they have leapt forward again to several forms of superiority. (2) Soviet *theater* nuclear weapons have placed European cities under the threat of almost instant annihilation through the SS-20s. (3) Soviet *conventional* forces have reached virtual qualitative parity with Western conventional forces, while retaining enormous advantages in the quantities of tanks, aircraft, and artillery pieces.[27]

The balance of power has been dramatically shifted by these advances. Many forms of military initiative have now passed into Soviet hands. They act; the West reacts.

If one looks at the planet strategically, observing the key pressure points, Soviet assets have grown steadily. The Soviet navy now maintains fleets in the South China Sea (with bases in Vietnam), in the Indian Ocean, and in the Mediterranean Sea, where Western shipping was earlier unchallenged. Moreover, the Soviets maintain armed nuclear submarines near both coasts of the United States and in the Caribbean (with bases in Cuba). The Soviet capacity to cut Africa off from America in the South Atlantic is also growing steadily. Finally, Soviet air and naval power in the North Atlantic is now so great that U.S. bases in Iceland and Greenland scarcely block their southward thrust. In virtually every theater, the Soviets have assets where they never had them before.

How shall we interpret the Soviet emphasis on military growth? Those who speak of "peacemaking" try to minimize it. This is the geopolitical context within which the Catholic Bishops have spoken. It is obvious that the Bishops pay scant attention to the changed quantity and quality, location and activities, of Soviet armed power. In calling for "an end to the arms race" the Bishops do not assess the present balance of power or its recent sharp shifts. They judge that peace will become more likely if the United States cuts back military spending and continues on its relative decline vis-à-vis Soviet power. They mention no "present danger" from Soviet arms growth.

One day, in the not too distant future, the advance of Soviet military power may nonetheless awaken the American public as never before. At that point, even the Bishops will discover how weak, relative to Soviet military power, U.S. power has become. The Soviets now have both the strategic potential, which they never had before, and the structural proclivities, of which over the years they have given ample evidence, to expand their military control over any one of many new targets of opportunity. Already in Central America, there is an active legion of East German, Bulgarian, Czech, Russian, Cuban, Libyan and PLO combatants. To the brigade of Russian combat troops in Cuba may one day be added other brigades in Nicaragua and elsewhere, together with Soviet missile crews and nuclear-armed aircraft. As the subversion of Costa Rica, Panama, El Salvador, Honduras and Guatemala proceeds, one can realistically imagine Soviet bases throughout Central America by 1990. By then, U.S. supply lines to Europe via the Caribbean will be cut off.

Nor is it difficult to imagine that, by 1990, Iran and Iraq may join Afghanistan as forward bases for Soviet aircraft, intelligence units, and rapid deployment forces.

With adroit boldness, Soviet leadership might also renegotiate the borders of Poland and East Germany, expanding East German control over the poorly performing industrial cities of Western Poland. They would do this to bring "Polish living standards up to East German levels, in genuine solidarity." Simultaneously, they might remove large portions of the Berlin Wall, offering West Germans free access to their relatives in East Germany in exchange for West German withdrawal from NATO. Without formal reunification, West and East Germany would be pressured to sign pacts committing both to "disarmament" and "neutralization," to heightened economic trade and political cooperation. Soviet military power would ensure the Swedenization of the strongest nation in NATO.

Moreover, a rising genius in the Soviet military might well argue that the worldwide "correlation of forces" is more in favor of the USSR than it has ever been, or is likely to be in the future, and that, before the current weapons systems became obsolete they ought to be used to ensure Soviet security for generations to come—by seizing the oil fields of the Middle East, the Rynkin Islands north of Japan, and Pakistan; but, first, by breaking the spirit of NATO.

The strategic calculation would run as follows: Soviet ICBMs have now neutralized the American strategic deterrent. No U.S. leader will commit U.S. cities to destruction in order to defend Europe. The Soviets could, therefore, force Western Europe to capitulate in one of two ways. The most daring way would be to destroy one European city—perhaps Hamburg—with a sudden rain of SS-20s. All other cities would be alerted to imminent follow-up, unless a negotiated armistice were immediately entered into. According to the U.S. Catholic Bishops, no nuclear retaliation by the West would be morally permissible; in any case, no retaliation would be likely. Citizens in the U.S. would be loathe to have the scenes from Hamburg, witnessed on television, repeated in Minneapolis-St. Paul. The Soviets would offer a nonaggression pact, holding Soviet troops out of Western Europe. All they would ask in exchange is European disarmament.

In Europe, many on the left already champion European neutralism. Political pressure in this direction would be strengthened by the overwhelming military power of the Soviets, poised for further destruction.

Once Europe had preemptively surrendered in the largest matter, year by year many smaller surrenders would be demanded. Anti-Soviet publications would be considered violations of neutrality. Broadcasting services to Eastern Europe—the Vatican, the BBC, Radio Free Europe—would be banned. Anything violating Soviet sovereignty and privilege would be punished. Leaders from European Communist parties would be favored as the most appropriate representatives to send to Moscow for the conduct of trade and other matters. Without being occupied, Western Europe would be humiliated in every possible small way. Waves of assassinations of anti-peace leaders would routinely occur and routinely be "deplored" by Moscow. American companies in Europe would be nationalized if possible, often expelled. Anti-American propaganda would gain intensity. The European media would be restricted to friends of peace, neutrality and solidarity.

This is one scenario. Another would be more brutal. Intent on demonstrating that the Red Army is invincible, the bold Soviet general staff would unleash its full fury on the Northern German Plain, warning that resort to tactical nuclear weapons by NATO would be met by the swift destruction of one city after another by SS-20s. Following Soviet battle doctrine, the Red Army would strike in massed formations, wave after wave, breaking through thin NATO defenses at will in three selected corridors, aiming to reach the Rhine within three weeks. The Red Sword would not seek to subjugate but to cut the spine of resistance, knowing that fleeing refugees would clog every highway with millions of personal automobiles, making effective reinforcement by conventional arms hopeless. Modern cities being easier than ancient cities to paralyze, ten thousand intelligence offices now under deep cover in Western Germany would move to assigned assaults upon communications and information systems. Almost as swiftly as General Jaruzelski broke the back of Solidarity in a single night, West Germany would be stricken.

The airlift capacities of the United States are currently so low, and reinforcements of troops at the ready so few, that military assistance from the United States could not arrive in time. The negotiated nonaggression pact would provide that all American forces humbly disembark within thirty days.

The lesson to the world would be stark. If NATO cannot resist the Red Army, can Pakistan, Iran, or Saudi Arabia? Can Israel? Concessions everywhere would flow toward Moscow.

It is obvious that such scenarios are problematic. I use them for purposes of illustration. The Catholic Bishops of the U.S. may have read the "signs of the time" correctly. But history may judge them guilty of immense miscalculations.

For talking of peace is a proven Leninist tactic; when the Soviets prepare for war (as in Afghanistan) they invariably launch a "peace offensive."[28] Talking of peace is cheap; and it easily feeds illusions and complacence. It may also lack deterrent force, suggesting a readiness to surrender without a fight. It may, as it often has, quicken brutal instincts.

Inadequate Deterrence

The Bishops are eager to confine the use of nuclear weapons solely to their function of deterrence. This is the truly great moral imperative of our age: to deter each and every unjust use of nuclear weapons, whether as explosives or as forces of unjust intimidation. But if this is the overriding moral imperative, then those who weaken deterrence incur the gravest of all contemporary responsibilities.

By definition, deterrence is successful only so long as the actual use of nuclear weapons is deterred. Thus, the strictures of the Bishops against various forms of *use* of nuclear weapons aim only at those cases in which deterrence has broken down. The moral imperative is to keep deterrence intact. The question on which moral guidance is desperately needed is as follows: *What must we Americans do to make certain that deterrence works?* On this crucial matter, the Bishops are silent.

The French word for deterrence is *dissuasion*. This word captures the psychological, human dimension better than the English. It focuses our attention on the human beings who need to be dissuaded. The Soviet leaders are a relatively small band. They consist of Yuri Andropov, the fourteen members of the Soviet Politburo (the Soviet "Fourteen Families"), key generals, the top officers of the KGB, and the top echelon of the Communist Party USSR. To discern how to dissuade these few, one must analyze their strategic assets, their proclivities, and their lived doctrines. How solid and convincing are such men likely to find the present American deterrent force? What do they see as American weaknesses? What are the weak places in the American mind?

For many years, the American nuclear force was unmatched by Soviet nuclear power. During that period, American nuclear power offered a cheap, moral, humane "umbrella" blocking superior Soviet conventional forces in Europe. In recent years, however, that umbrella has become porous. It is not psychologically believable that an American President will order U.S. strategic nuclear forces to answer a Soviet attack, nuclear or conventional, upon Europe. Such an order would be suicidal for U.S. urban centers. If Americans of fifty years ago shouted "We won't die for Danzig," neither will those of today die for Hamburg. The Soviet nuclear build-up has for the time being effectively decoupled Europe from America.

Furthermore, as the realization spreads that the U.S. "nuclear umbrella" no longer covers Europe, the logic of maintaining 300,000 U.S. troops in Europe is undercut. For a Soviet attack upon Europe, conventional or nuclear, would now hold these young men and women, and their families, hostage. Indeed, a craftily designed Soviet nuclear attack upon Europe—of the admonitory, limited sort mentioned above—would seek to avoid involving American forces. Its aim would be to decouple the fate of America from that of Europe, and to give passion to the cry: "Americans out of Europe!"

Should it become clear, in the meantime, that the Europeans were unwilling to build up a sufficient *conventional* deterrent, so that American troops would be hostages to a doomed conventional defense, this fact, too, would place the President of the U.S. in an impossible position. Serious analysts are already advising the U.S. to withdraw these newly vulnerable "hostages to fortune" from the danger zone.

From the point of view of strategic Soviet interests, the decoupling of European security from American security has been a brilliant political achievement. This political achievement rests upon the three-part military achievement of acquiring (1) at least parity with the U.S. in strategic systems; (2) at least temporary superiority in theater nuclear forces (the SS-20s); and (3) virtual *qualitative* parity with NATO forces in conventional weaponry, while retaining immense *quantitative* advantages. Whichever way NATO turns, it is vulnerable.

This shift in the balance of power has weakened deterrence. A weakened deterrent increases the probabilities of a breakdown in deterrence. Although they claim to be seeking peace, the Catholic Bishops said nothing to address this present danger. Although they condemned most uses of nuclear weapons, their failure to strengthen the present leaky deterrent raises the probabilities of an aggressive, limited use of nuclear weapons by the Soviets.

Those concerned about making deterrence work need moral guidance.

(1) What is the *just cause* of all the effort, expense and moral discipline required to make deterrence effective? Put another way, what is the

theological value of Western *institutions?* Some theologians, in fact, hold these institutions relatively cheap. They point out that Christian values *transcend* any worldly institutions. Christians can live Christian lives, they say, even if Western institutions perish. Are Western institutions of such low theological value, then, that they should not be defended? There are passages in the Bishops' Letter suggesting such a surrender. These are the most intellectually and morally disgraceful passages in the Bishops' Letter.[29] One is left wondering whether the Bishops side with Pius IX's condemnation of liberal institutions in his "Syllabus of Errors." This cannot be true. Still, by leaving the relation of Catholic faith to the institutions of a liberal society in question, the Bishops omit the just cause.

(2) Can free societies make sacrifices for self-defense decade after decade? Deterrence is much less expensive than a breakdown of deterrence would be. In particular, nuclear deterrence is less than one-tenth as expensive as conventional deterrence. From 1962 to 1982, the U.S. spent, on average, $21 billion per year on nuclear arms, about ten percent of the military budget, or about one-half percent of GNP.[30] Deterrent systems, based on material mechanisms, wear out and become obsolete; their useful life is, typically, about fifteen years. (The retirement of such systems unused is the clearest possible evidence of their moral purpose.) For this reason, a generational cycle of expenses must be anticipated, as a matter of material necessity. This cycle is again upon us in the 1980s.

Furthermore, each new generational cycle affords fresh opportunities for the invention of new designs of superior moral standing. Thus, in the 1950s, the first generation of heavy, relatively inaccurate weapons could plausibly be aimed only at cities. Proportionality and discrimination were out of the question. This led to the least moral nuclear doctrine, Mutual Assured Destruction. In the late 1960s, the second generation of nuclear weapons permitted much smaller warheads on missiles of far greater accuracy. This new technology permitted "Flexible Response," or the targeting of military objectives. Morally speaking, this is an advance. For the coming third generation, it is now possible to imagine still smaller warheads of still greater accuracy, on a scale approximate to that of the larger conventional weapons.

Here moral guidance is necessary. Would such new technologies have a superior moral character, by their more reasonable proportion and more discriminating capabilities?[31] Or should they be rejected, because they diminish the psychological distance between conventional and nuclear arms? The Bishops, as we have seen, seem to take this second position. I believe this is an error in moral judgment.

(3) Strategic deterrence until now has been focused on *offensive* weapons systems. From these arise both the moral repugnance generated by Mutual Assured Destruction and the quite ancient questions about proportionality and discrimination. Technological investigation aimed at

developing *defensive* systems, which would render ballistic and other offensive weapons obsolete, seems to afford several moral advantages. First, defensive systems conform better to the right to self-defense. Second, they might lift the terrible threat of sudden offensive attack, a threat endured now for more than thirty years. Third, the secrets of defensive deterrence could plausibly be shared with one's foes, since such secrets constitute no offensive threat.

Moral leaders should encourage new types of strategic thinking. The Bishops do not.

(4) Examining the weak links in the American (and Allied) deterrent systems, moral leaders ought to support the efforts, expenses and moral disciplines necessary to repair those weaknesses, lest deterrence break down. Those who do not want to see nuclear war *must* do everything necessary to deter it. If the West has been complacent, the Bishops should sound a clarion call. If the present is a moment of danger, the Bishops should summon up courage and will. Instead of summoning the American people to the sacrifices necessary to redress the current imbalance of power, however, the Bishops have assumed that there is no imbalance. Perhaps they are correct. But evidence seems overwhelming that theirs is a grave intellectual and moral misjudgment.

The actions of the Soviet Union will soon enough clarify which of the two visions of reality is true: that the long Soviet struggle to obtain a correlation of forces (strategic, theater and conventional) favorable to the USSR places the West in mortal danger; or that American Catholics best acquit their moral and intellectual responsibilities by practicing nuclear disarmament, lowering expenditures on arms, and appealing to love.

It will be better for all of us if the Bishops are correct and I am wrong. But I am fearful that the reverse is true. Just when the West needed a call to disciplined deterrence, the net geopolitical impact of the Bishops' letter was to contribute to illusions. The Bishops did resist pacifism; that is to their credit. They did not, despite much activism, destroy deterrence; that, too, is to their credit. But they failed to strengthen the clarity of soul necessary to make deterrence work, and that marks a grave religious as well as political failure.

NOTES

1. "A Vatican Synthesis," *Origins* 12 (April 7, 1983), p. 695. This Vatican memorandum to the U.S. Bishops codifies the points discussed at a meeting at the Vatican Secretariat of State, January 18–19, 1981, attended by several European and U.S. Bishops.

2. "Where Bomb-making is Big Business," *Life* (July 1982), p. 67. The Bishop appears on the cover astride a white horse.

3. Gordon Oliver, "Seattle Bishop Tells of Plans to Resist Taxes," *National Catholic Reporter* (February 5, 1982).

4. On the Soviet campaign, see Vladimir Bukovsky, "The Peace Movement and the Soviet Union," *Commentary* 73 (May 1982), pp. 25–41; and Rael Jean Isaac and Erich Isaac, "The Counterfeit Peacemakers: Atomic Freeze," *American Spectator* 15 (June 1982), pp. 8–17.

5. In private discussions, June 8, 1983.

6. Albert Wohlstetter, "Bishops, Statesmen, and Other Strategists on the Bombing of Innocents," *Commentary* 75 (June 1983), p. 31.

7. "The pastoral letter fully deserves the audience it seeks. It is a thoughtful and comprehensive effort to bring religious and moral principles to bear on nuclear weapons. In reaching their conclusions, the bishops have been unafraid to criticize existing official positions; in turn they have been treated first with suspicion and then with wary assertions of sympathy by the Reagan administration. The pervading concern of their letter is with the 'unique challenge' presented by nuclear warfare to 'the classical Christian position' on war and peace. The power of their response to this challenge makes the report a landmark in the changing pattern of American concern with nuclear danger, and an excellent starting point for a look at what can now be said about deterrence." McGeorge Bundy, "The Bishops and the Bomb," *New York Review of Books* (June 16, 1983), p. 3.

8. Patty Edmonds, "Bishops Commit Church to Peace," *National Catholic Reporter* (May 13, 1983), p. 19.

9. "The Bishops Speak Out," *National Review* (June 10, 1983), pp. 674–81.

10. "A Vatican Synthesis," pp. 694–95.

11. Aleksandr Solzhenitsyn, *Warning to the West* (New York: Farrar, Straus and Giroux, 1976), pp. 76–77.

12. Bishop Leroy Matthiesen has said, "The Catholic Church is on a direct collision course with the United States government, and I'll be right out there taking the brunt of it." "Where Bomb-making Is Big Business," p. 67.

13. "In support of the concept of 'sufficiency' as an adequate deterrent and in light of the present size and composition of both U.S. and Soviet strategic arsenals, we recommend: support for immediate, bilateral, verifiable agreements to halt the testing, production and deployment of new nuclear systems." National Conference of Catholic Bishops, *The Challenge of Peace: God's Promise and Our Response* (Washington, D.C.: United States Catholic Conference, 1983), II, D2, 191.

14. *Ibid.*, II, C2, 153.

15. *Ibid.*, 156.

16. *Ibid.*, II, D2, 184.

17. *Ibid.*, 192.

18. *Ibid.*, 190.

19. Salvador de Madaviaga, chairman of the League of Nations Disarmament Commission and Disarmament Conference, speaking in 1973. Quoted in Barbara W. Tuchman, "The Alternative to Arms Control," *New York Times Magazine* (April 18, 1982), p. 98. Miss Tuchman also writes after chronicling the various unsuccessful efforts at arms control: "I have engaged in this long and dreary survey in order to show that control of war in the form of disarmament or limitation of arms has been a fruitless effort" (p. 93).

20. Theodore Draper, "How Not to Think About Nuclear War," *New York Review of Books* (July 16, 1982), p. 42. Commenting on the celebrated no-first-use proposal of McGeorge Bundy, George F. Kennan, Robert S. McNamara and Gerard

Smith (*Foreign Affairs*, Spring 1982), Draper adds: "If a declaration of peaceful intentions were enough to prevent any kind of war, the deed would have been done a long time ago. The history of war and peace is littered with such professions of virtue. In 1928, for example, sixty-two nations signed a pact outlawing war. Its enforcement was supposed to rest on the moral strength of world opinion. It was signed, celebrated, and forgotten. With evident understatement, the four authors themselves say that 'such declarations may have only limited reliability.' The awful truth is that they have no reliability at all" (p. 35).

21. The ABM treaty is sometimes cited. But the result of that treaty is that the USSR has built up its one permissible ABM system in the Moscow region, protecting not only its capital but some seventy percent of its missile force; the U.S. does not deploy an ABM system. The Soviets gain battlefield advantages as readily through negotiations as through actual war.

22. Testimony of Hon. David A. Stockman, Director, Office of Management and Budget, before the Joint Economic Committee, U.S. Congress, May 4, 1983.

23. For numbers of strategic bombers see Kevin N. Lewis, *The Economics of SALT Revisited* (Santa Monica, Calif.: Rand Corp., 1979), p. 13; and *The Military Balance 1982–83* (London: International Institute for Strategic Studies, 1982), p. 4. Regarding the size of the U.S. nuclear arsenal, Secretary of Defense Caspar Weinberger notes: "We have fewer nuclear warheads today than we had in 1967— not a handful fewer but thousands fewer." See News Release No. 168-82 (April 20, 1982), Office of Assistant Secretary of Defense (Public Affairs). Although the exact number of nuclear warheads is classified, a careful student can deduce that, while the number of strategic warheads has remained relatively steady, the number of tactical warheads has declined, resulting in an overall reduction in the totality of the U.S. stockpile since 1965. Some deductions reveal that the throwweight of the U.S. strategic missile force has declined by half in the past decade-and-a-half.

24. See Michael Charlton, "The Eagle and the Small Birds: The Spectre of Yalta," *Encounter* 60 (June 1982), pp. 7–28.

25. Thus, at SALT I, U.S. negotiators concentrated on limiting launchers, which are easier to verify. This gave impetus to MIRVed launchers, multiplying the number of warheads on each. The search for objects easily and certainly verifiable consistently distorts negotiations.

26. The figures are Solzhenitsyn's, as reported in Edward E. Ericson, Jr., *Solzhenitsyn: The Moral Vision* (Grand Rapids, Mich.: William B. Eerdmans, 1980), p. 151. For the number of Communist dominated countries, see *CIR Report*, Washington, D.C.: Center for International Relations, July 1983), p. 2.

27. *Has America Become No. 2?* (Washington, D.C.: Committee on the Present Danger, 1982), pp. 28–9. See also *The Military Balance 1982–1983*, pp. 132–33.

28. See Bukovsky, "The Peace Movement and the Soviet Union."

29. "Nonviolent resistance, like war, can take many forms depending upon the demands of a given situation. There is, for instance, organized popular defense instituted by government as part of its contingency planning. Citizens would be trained in the techniques of peaceable noncompliance and noncooperation as a means of hindering an invading force or nondemocratic government from imposing its will. Effective nonviolent resistance requires the united will of a people and may

demand as much patience and sacrifice from those who practice it as is now demanded by war and preparation for war. It may not always succeed. Nevertheless, before the possibility is dismissed as impractical or unrealistic, we urge that it be measured against the almost certain effects of a major war." NCCB, *Challenge of Peace*, III A, 5, 223.

30. *National Defense Budget Estimates for FY 1984*, Office of the Assistant Secretary of Defense (Comptroller), March 1983, p. 62.

31. I accept here the argument of Albert Wohlstetter, cited above.

Francis X. Meehan

Nonviolence and the Bishops' Pastoral: A Case for a Development of Doctrine

Father Meehan teaches theology at Immaculata College, Immaculata, Pennsylvania, and is the author of *A Contemporary Social Spirituality* (Orbis Press).

Introduction: The Thesis

The central thesis of this chapter is that the Church is moving and, I believe, must move to such a realistic evaluation of modern war that for all practical purposes it will become a Church of nonviolence.[1] The chapter attempts to explain what Thomas Merton once claimed, that he could theoretically hold for the doctrine of the just war, but that given the concrete conditions of modern war he found it necessary to be a pacifist.[2] Notice, of course, how this is a play on the usual slogan which claims that it is only just-war teaching which is practical and realistic. Merton stood the point on its head and asked us to see it entirely the other way. Such is my purpose as well.

This essay reflects on a development of doctrine within the Church. But even at the outset it is important to note that a development can occur in quite indirect ways. For example, Karl Rahner has given examples of how between Catholic and Protestants there may be continued opposition in theory and yet some convergence in practice.[3] A recent case in point occurred when the American Bishops condemned capital punishment. They spoke this opposition to capital punishment not on doctrinaire grounds but on the conviction that in its present application capital punishment would never be able to be administered equitably and justly.[4] Thus our imagination is provoked to consider that there could be an historical situation in which the Church, while theoretically affirming the right to use force for self-defense or defense of a country, nevertheless chooses to deny the right in practice in the face of realities which render force immoderate and indiscriminate. Thus a development of doctrine can be imagined which would maintain continuity in certain dimensions of a moral value, in spite of a real shift in the practical norm—not unlike what occurred in the Church's history regarding the issue of usury.

This is precisely one of the key points this chapter will make regarding the relationship between just-war teaching and nonviolence. When we engage in discussion as to where the Church should be on these two issues, sometimes it seems as if the arguments could go on forever. There seems to be no solution. There is especially no way out of the dilemma if we argue only from our head. But we are called to live life not merely inside our heads, but to live life concretely. And when we begin to leave the pure abstract logic of the head, we are forced to confront the concrete living reality of how war is becoming more and more brutal, the killing more and more widespread.[5]

The person defending the just-war teaching will often insist that despite such increased brutality, the teaching remains valid since it is the teaching itself which condemns the disproportionate and the indiscriminate aspect of the killing.[6] Yet somehow one must look again. One must look to see how indiscriminate killing seems to be becoming an integral part of modern warmaking.[7] There comes a time when we must reexamine the just-war teaching. It is not that the teaching would become invalid simply by being violated so frequently. On the contrary, the teaching remains all the more valid. Its very principles, which require moderation and discrimination, enable us to point to the evil of indiscriminate killing and to name it as evil. And to point to an evil and to name something as evil is to help us take a fresh look at all war today and at the meaning of war not only in theory but also in the concrete. It was the just-war teaching itself which became the catalyst for Vatican II to call for an "entirely new attitude."[8]

Thus the just-war principles themselves, especially those of discriminacy and proportion, if we look at them closely and concretely, may help us to move to the necessity of a total rejection of war, and thus to a moral posture of nonviolence. In order to reflect on how such an evolution of teaching can take place, I wish first to express profound appreciation for what the American Bishops have said about the relationship between nonviolence and just-war teaching. They clearly have not demanded a total church posture of nonviolence. This essay, while written in appreciation, nevertheless suggests that the Bishops' Pastoral constitutes only one stage in an ongoing development of doctrine, and by no means the last stage.[9]

I wish to be clear that throughout this essay I am using "nonviolence" and "pacifism" in an interchangeable way even though there can be different historical interpretations;[10] and I take as a definition of "violence" Karl Rahner's concept, namely, the use of physical means "which do not address themselves to the insight and freedom of the other—when it intervenes in the sphere of another, to act on it and change it without its previous consent."[11]

The Pastoral's Teaching

Let us begin by stating exactly just how the Bishops' Pastoral sees the relationship between just-war teaching and nonviolence. The Pastoral's claim is that between the two there exists a "complementary relationship in the sense that both seek to serve the common good."[12] The Bishops repeat this thought in various ways, for example, claiming that the "new moment" in which they find themselves sees the just-war teaching and nonviolence "as distinct but interdependent methods of evaluating warfare . . . " They add that the "two perspectives support and complement one another, each preserving the other from distortion."[13]

It is clear that the Bishops recognize nonviolence as holding an authentic place in Catholic tradition, though naturally not the only place. This very recognition is itself somewhat of a development of doctrine in that the acknowledgment of nonviolence as a genuine option is not easy to find in most moral manuals, and does not seem to have been in Pius XII's teaching, to name one modern Pope.[14] Even Vatican II's praise of nonviolence was given with the proviso that "this can be done without injury to the rights and duties of others or of the community itself."[15] While the Pastoral refers to this last qualification of Vatican II, its recognition of nonviolence as a legitimate tradition is so frequent and consistent that one can say that the nonviolent option is legitimized here in a way unprecedented for any such authoritative Church document.[16]

The very significant terms I have mentioned, namely, "two distinct moral responses" and "complementary relationship," speak a language which at the very least recognizes nonviolence as having an authentic place in Catholic tradition. This, however, does not nullify the Bishops' endorsement of just-war teaching. It is especially when the Bishops dialogue with public policy that they carefully apply just war criteria. In Chapter Two of the Pastoral they take a clear position against any actual use of nuclear weapons; they reach this conclusion not through an appeal to pacifism, but through a simple and careful application of the just-war principles of *proportionality* and *just conduct*. It is precisely through the very just war teaching that the Bishops show how nuclear war in the actual world in which we live could never claim to be a truly just war.[17]

When examining what the Bishops did say about the relationship between nonviolence and just war teaching, and noting that they did use the words "complementary relationship," we should be wary of a certain danger which such a phrase could invite, namely, the danger of a certain imprecision as to the meaning of the term "complementary." Obviously, just-war teaching and nonviolence cannot be totally complementary. One allows killing and the other does not. We must be wary of a false liberalism which waters down the full strength of nonviolence. We have to be wary of a form of pluralism which would imply that all things are easily reconcilable. This would be to lose an eschatological pull of the Gospel disclosure of Jesus' teaching and life which clearly resists any use of violence.[18] Therefore any vision which sees just-war teaching and nonviolence as complementary should at least not be an easy and casual integration. Indeed, the Bishops' document should be seriously questioned on this point. Were they too quickly covering over real differences between the just war choice and the nonviolent choice by simply summing them up as "choices for the Kingdom"?[19] I do not pretend to resolve this issue here. Rather I am making a more modest proposal, only that there are *certain dimensions* to the just-war teaching which can be seen as complementary to nonviolence, and in fact can even evolve into a Church posture of nonviolence once one examines the concrete reality of warmaking today.

Questions Concerning a Development of Doctrine

If since modern war seems so intrinsically savage and unrestrained, just war teaching is gradually seen as less and less useful, and if this diminished usefulness results in a certain development of doctrine, what would such a development look like theologically? How do we go about even phrasing the question correctly since it is a question which touches on so many aspects of theology, of grace and sin, of church and world, of law and Gospel? I would like to pause a moment to ask a series of questions in order to hint at the scope of the theological issues involved. This chapter does not propose to answer these questions but only to put them into a context which can hopefully release our imaginations. I would propose three sets of questions, the first touching on the nature of nonviolence, the second on the ecclesiological issue involved, and the third set on the more properly theological aspect of the question.

Any lengthy inquiry would first have to ask the meaning of nonviolence and how it may be comparable with the pacifism of the early Church. Must the nonviolence of which we speak in this development be entirely pure to be called a true development? Or could we speak of a social pacifism that refuses only war, without thereby implying that a father would have to stand by to see his children attacked by a neighborhood bully. Can there, for example, be degrees of nonviolence which leave some place for police protection and coercive force at levels lower than war between nation-states?

A second set of questions touches on the ecclesiological problems of what models of Church and what relationship with the world a nonviolent posture would imply. The ecclesiological question also touches on exactly what authority can be claimed in Catholic tradition for a nonviolent option. How can the Bishops justify their claim when they say that "the just-war teaching has clearly been in possession for the last 1500 years of Catholic thought"?[20] On what basis now does the Church maintain a nation's right to go to war? Could the Church ever reach a point at which such a claim would look something like the Syllabus of Errors' concept of democracy, when it is placed against Vatican II's *Declaration on Religious Liberty*?[21] Would any development of doctrine require that the understanding of the very legitimacy of the nation-state be changed, just as the very meaning of money changed in the Renaissance and just as the very meaning of state changed in the nineteenth and twentieth centuries so as to demand a different articulation of Church and State in the *Declaration on Religious Liberty*?

Indeed, if acceptance of nonviolence could be imagined as a development in the Church, just as the movement against slavery developed, how would we expect that to come about? Surely not cleanly from the top down, surely not without struggles, not without some unevenness of vision for a time, not without pockets of resistance, not without some feeling that the development was in fact a betrayal of Church teaching. Has this not been the case in other areas of development of doctrine?

A third set of questions concerns the properly theological dimension of the question. If followers of Jesus discover that physical violence ought not to be used to defend a cause or a people, how would we begin to understand the meaning of such an ethic? The answer would surely be more than deontologic, that is, more than merely an extrinsic or literalist obedience to an ethical command. Rather we would have to pierce through to the why of the new ethical imperative itself and how it relates to realities of faith such as redemption and salvation.

It would have to include a question about the meaning of suffering in this world, and about the connection of justice in this world with justice in the final Kingdom. Our inquiry would have to try to understand the meaning of pluralism at its starkest point, that is, why in this world there is more than one opinion, one way, one ideology, and how we deal with the *other* way, the *other* person, the *irreducible* other, even when that other constitutes *harm* for myself or my people.

Simply to mention these questions is enough, I hope, to enable us to see the issue of nonviolence vs. just war teaching in larger perspective than mere ethical casuistry. To avoid this trap of narrow thinking, the following sections will attempt to place the question of a Church development toward nonviolence in three larger contexts: the context of "duality," the context of sin and grace, and the context of the dialectic of evil in the world.

Placing the "Development" in the Context of Duality

To imagine how the Church could develop toward a doctrinal position of nonviolence would mean getting out somehow from under the imposing dilemma as it now presents itself. After all, the Bishops' statement itself uses that startling term "complementary relationship"—startling in that non-violence and just-war teaching seem to be sharply opposed. How can nonviolence and violence be complementary? How can the willingness to kill and the refusal to do so be interdependent? I propose the concept of duality in order to resolve this dilemma.[22] But first allow me to describe a personal but, I believe, common experience as an illustration of the meaning of moving from dilemma to duality.

Whenever I am discussing nonviolence and just war, I notice that a certain restlessness sets in among even the most committed people. I have found that an inevitable dialectic develops. Even among peace activists and people committed to nonviolence, the purity of their commitment to nonviolence is very often tested and thrown into doubt by the proposal of certain historical situations where the use of force is so clearly rational.

This leads to a suspicion that just war and nonviolence may be part of something deeper than the usual casuistic argument between two alternatives to handling conflict. This deeper reality I call a duality. By this I mean simply that we are up against two modes of action which cannot be resolved into one on their own plane. I am not speaking of dualism or monism, but of duality, that is, there will always be the two, at least in theory, and they will neither be necessarily stark opposites nor will they collapse totally into one answer. For there to be any true development away from the dilemma of just war or nonviolence, something wider than the two issues will have to intervene to allow resolution.

Indeed, I suspect, a duality of nonviolence-and-just war is connected with some other classic issues of duality. One thinks immediately of the first and last duality which the human mind confronts, the issue of the *One*-and-the-*many*. The mind cannot rest on the One without soon being confronted with the *many*. One cannot live with the many without striving for some synthesis, some unity. Sin-and-grace are similar dualities in Christian history. One's mind cannot finally settle on which the human is, sinful or grace-filled, without being confronted with the other reality. Justice-and-peace is another duality even more closely and obviously connected. These dualities have always prevented a certain resting of the mind. This is clearly the case with our own issue. For just-war teaching concerns the use of a physically coercive force in a sinful world, while nonviolence appeals more explicitly to a graced freedom.

For the Christian who reads the Scriptures, it is difficult to rest with the use of a physical force that maims and kills the human body. Yet it can also be difficult for the same Christian to rest with perfect nonviolence in the face of so many injustices and brutalities visited upon the innocent. Not only the mind, but also the heart, is unable to rest in one or the other. This context of duality is helpful because it makes us aware of the greater depth of the issue. It allows for the emergence of a certain humility. The longer one thinks on these issues the more one realizes that quick rational arguments about the rightness and wrongness of a particular action simply do not exhaust the issue. Rather we begin to realize that we are in the middle of a very deep human tension between two great realities, a realization that quickly undermines any easy presumption of "rightness."

The point about two elements of a duality is that they exercise upon each other a living tension, a claim to recognize reciprocal influence. Let me put it most simply. I am suggesting that the witness of nonviolence makes the use of just-war teachings more just and honest. In other words, the witness of refusing to use force has a power in the world which tends to reduce the use of force and to assure a more moderate and just application of whatever force is used. And the very power of the nonviolent witness enables the just-war teaching to be applied rigorously, ultimately leading the Church into a *practical* posture of nonviolence.

There is a corollary to this which I will only touch upon lightly in this chapter, namely, that the just-war teaching's intent and value act in turn as a moderating influence upon the witness of nonviolence. In other words, any effort at Gospel purity must always have a certain down-to-earth-ness, lest the purity itself assume certain demonic tendencies.[23] I will leave this point undeveloped here. For the moment I am more concerned with how nonviolence is becoming an increasingly significant witness, and I believe, a more necessary witness. This is evident when one places just-war teaching in a context of sin and grace.

The Context of Sin and Grace and a Development of Doctrine

To imagine how the Church could develop toward a posture of nonviolence, it would be important to place the Bishops' concept of "complementary" within a theology of sin and grace. Only by grounding the word "complementary" in a solid concept of grace and sin will we be able to understand how there could be a real development of doctrine.[24] Let us examine first Karl Rahner's teaching on the meaning of force in a graced yet sinful world. Basically, his teaching holds that force must always be reaching out to become nonforce. That is, if just-war teaching is not reaching toward less and less violence, it will end up acquiescing in the violation of its very own criteria.[25] Rahner develops a central theological assertion about the use of force: "this sort of power ought never to have existed."[26] Thus force is seen as an activity that stems from sin, though every use of force need not represent an actual sin, a position Rahner carefully distinguishes from what he calls a "Protestant understanding of the human."

He compares the use of force to certain other "natural" things such as suffering and death. They are comparable in that they should not exist either, but they do and once given, can be seen as something human to be used well; unfortunately, they can also be abused. The key to their correct use or abuse is whether or not they become integrated into the human or are left unintegrated.[27] To help us here, Rahner places force within the theological category of "concupiscence". And his understanding of concupiscence is something larger than the frequent moral use of the term. It is not a mere moral temptation urging us to evil, but something deeper and all embracing, the very inability of human beings "to integrate fully and clearly the whole reality of (their) existence."[28]

To put force into this category helps us to see it as something which is always less than ideal because it is always appealing for more and more integration into human freedom. Rahner is being realistic here but not with the same kind of realism which justifies the use of force simply by appealing to a sinful world and then stops there. There is realism too when the Bishops and the Council claim that "governments cannot be denied the right to legitimate defense."[29] But if we stop there, we have missed the meaning of a genuine theological realism. In other words, if we simply quote this abstract affirmation of government's right to legitimate defense, we are no longer seeing force as part of the concupiscent world which stems from sin. In this way force becomes a static reality, and then one gives it a blank check, a kind of assumption of perfect rightness, with nothing to be mourned, regretted, or feared, with no ambiguity.

One can say, of course, that such a blank check is not just-war teaching at its best since, at its best, it is always an effort to restrain evil. But we must ask ourselves when do we ever see just-war teaching applied at its best concretely? It is precisely not at its best because it is rarely rooted in a theology of sin and grace in a truly *concrete* way. True, the flag of original sin is often waved as justification for the need for force or war, but often the moral conclusion of the right to go to war seems more a mathematical conclusion bereft of any sustained theology. One does not hear in the easy appeals to just war anything faintly resembling a real discernment of spirits concerning the dense historical question of how much force is allowable in the progressive effort at integration. Contrary to the usual accusations against the pacifist, it is just-war analysis which is often heady and abstract: "we may go to war if the following criteria are fulfilled. *Atqui* the criteria are fulfilled. Therefore we may go to war . . ." No need for the subtle ambiguities of grace and sin and human integration here! And when just-war teachers become abstract, the way is open for the worst sort of barbarism. Witness modern war's increasing toll on civilians and the subtle blessings of torture presently being tolerated for the sake of the modern security state.

We can be grateful that the American Bishops' Pastoral surrounds its just-war analysis of Chapter II with some serious theologizing in earlier sections on Scripture and in the section entitled, "Kingdom and History" (Chapter I).[30] What is to be feared, however, is that these sections tend to be merely juxtaposed to, rather than truly integrated into, the just-war analysis. This does not mean that we are asking the Bishops to become sectarian in their public policy analysis by being too explicit in the use of theological terms such as grace and sin. My point is more subtle perhaps, but crucial. I am not asking that the Church abandon its healthy sense of natural law reasoning by which it can aptly dialogue with the public forum and by which it can recognize the wisdom of God in the human sciences.[31] Indeed, the American Bishops' use of just-war teaching and their application of it to public policy is, I believe, a real unveiling of the face of the Divine. For here they do allow for concrete application which would restrain any use of nuclear weapons because of their indiscriminate and disproportionate brutality.

With all this being said, however, there remains, in my opinion, too much room for a peculiar schizophrenia among Catholics. It is a schizophrenia that articulates one principle on paper but looks the other way when it comes to concrete application and the need for vigorous protest, indeed when it comes down to an actual explicit naming of an unjust policy.[32] This subtle nonapplication calls to mind a heresy which Rahner speaks of—he uses one of his favorite terms "crypto-heresy."[33] He is speaking of acquiescence in the use of force, an overlooking of its theological ambiguity, a failure to see it as a reality to be overcome by being progressively integrated into graced forms of love, reason, persuasion, freedom.

Rahner's words on the idea of a crypto-heresy are forceful and clear:

> Anyone who thought that force was the surest and simplest way, who held it was the most real thing and basically the only reliable feeling, who would make no attempt to abolish it and go beyond it, would be a secret heretic who had fallen away from the truth of Christianity, since he would refuse to admit that this force stems from sin . . . [34]

So we can admit that force is "possible and even justified in a world of blindness and passion where men are not free and not penetrated by divine truth." But he cautions that "it can only be *rightly* [emphasis his] used by someone who is aware of its danger and ambiguity." One cannot help but be reminded of Augustine's vision that only he who loves could dare to kill.[35]

While Rahner and Augustine's interpretation could, of course, be easily satirized for being too lax, inward, Platonic, individualistic, we must not allow ourselves to miss their great truth, namely, that the Christian doctrine of grace is subverted when we too easily assume that force is the "right" answer. This kind of "righteousness" has always plagued Catholic moral theology. It has often been said that our theology lost an eschatological tension.[36] In other words, we too easily bless those actions which a sinful world has forced upon us. We bless them as reasonable, as right. We quickly lose sight of their "nonkingdom-like" reality. In that sense we remove ourselves too easily from a tension which the final kingdom should be exercising upon us.

Indeed, to use Richard Niebuhr's phrase, Christ is thus absorbed by the culture rather than transforming it.[37] None of this happens, of course, in daylight. One hears complaints of the Latin American priest who picks up a gun and joins the guerrillas, and rightly so. But the danger in our American culture is more subtle. In North America, there is no temptation to pick up a gun. Our social situation is not so radicalized; the options are very different. But we must take a more careful look beneath the surface. Picking up a gun is not an issue for us, but we do have a certain social and political power as church—not just the priests among us. And as we failed to use that social power to speak out against the bombing of innocent civilians in past wars, so now too we can fail to use our power to speak out against forms of preparation for war that will violate just-war criteria. This is our equivalent of picking up a gun. It is not enough that a few words have been written on paper by Bishops; our protest against the increasing militarization must be sustained and vigorous, must pervade the whole Church, its structures, and its grass-roots organizations.[38]

This can happen only when there is some pull from an eschatological kingdom, some sense of grace, some awareness that force is an element of concupiscence which stems from sin, and which therefore must be moderated, diminished, progressively abolished. This kind of theological rooting of just-war teaching will put us in sympathetic dialogue with the pacifists who insist on total nonviolence. No longer will we see them in opposition, but rather only in tension. Only by wrestling with their message, only by catching the infection of their faith and their willingness to suffer in imitation of Jesus on the cross, will just-war teachers ever be able to remain truly authentic practitioners of their own criteria and not become, in their abstractness, unwitting supporters of modern militarism.[39] Thus, once we put just-war teaching in the context of a theology of sin and grace, we see how a new doctrine can develop in continuity with the old, and how there can be a progressive movement in the Church toward nonviolence, and finally how the two are not dichotomous but "complementary" realities.

The Development of Doctrine Seen in the Context of Evil's Dialectic

There is another way to show how there must be and indeed already is development of doctrine on the use of violence. One must study history and see how violence fails in the long run to solve issues. This is a context of Christian realism but again a different realism from the one usually invoked to justify force. In a particularly helpful study, Indian theologian Raimundo Pannikar situates his thought on nonviolence in the context of recognizing the "other" in our world.[40] How do we truly recognize the *other* and allow the *other* to be? It is only in learning this that we can begin to think of just war and nonviolence in a fruitful way.

Ultimately, he believes, we must learn the art of "dialogical tension rather than dialogical conflict."[41] In other words, one does not solve the problem of pluralism by forcing unity. But how can we let the *evil other* be? Pannikar does not have a magic answer here, but his reflection on the words of Jesus, "Do not resist evil," is extremely helpful. He calls this command of Jesus "one of the most daring sentences of Jesus' kerygma" and interprets it as meaning that we oppose evil but we do not "withstand the man who does evil." The reason: "Otherwise you will be drawn into the dialectical game;

you will have to build another power to oppose the first one, and so forth and so on. Thus from reaction to counter-reaction, from swing to counter-swing, we have the all too familiar pendular movement of the world.''[42]

Let us reflect on this insight for a moment. It makes nonviolence an insight of human wisdom rather than a fundamentalistic interpretation of Scripture, a principle for principle's sake, or a formal obedience to the commands of Jesus in the sense of a duty ethic. In this sense nonviolence exemplifies the opposite of the "deontologic" ethic. On the contrary, it becomes a concern for the realization of human purpose and, in that sense, it is more "teleologic."[43] Many easily assume that just-war teaching constitutes Christian realism; a long range look at nonviolence reveals its true realism.

In our modern world, given the way in which economic and political factors take sudden shifts, it is striking to see how young men can die for two opposing nation-states, only to find those same countries bonded together as allies a short time later. The repugnance we feel at young lives wasted constitutes a realistic, political and economic reason for valuing nonviolence. Pannikar sees in Jesus' commands an intrinsic political and socio-economic realism. This makes nonviolence more than an ethic of self-sacrifice, though I shall argue later that self-sacrifice does constitute the religious heart of the ethic. But Christians must grasp its human dimension as well.

Pannikar's interpretation has it that there is a form of resistance by which one is "drawn into the dialectical game . . . " He explains the dialectical game, saying:

> "God" was with the right, now "God" is with the left; at first the males dominated, now some females want to do the bossing; the colonial powers have exploited other peoples, now the other peoples are going to kick back with whatever arms they have at their disposal . . . and we go on and on and on.[44]

In other words, there is a form of resistance which inevitably brings contamination with the very evil one is resisting. The countries which went to war against Hitler's brutalities became immersed in the dialectic, eventually engaging in fire-bombing civilians themselves. We go "on and on and on." We build bigger and bigger bombs, more and more of them; in fact, some 17,000 new nuclear weapons have been projected for the next decade. We do this all the while "resisting the evil" of the other. Some realists are beginning to ask the question: Is there any end before our bombs destroy us all?[45] The pacifist then who demurs against resisting evil by violent means is indeed the most pragmatic, the true realist.

One of the most persuasive arguments in this regard can be found, I believe, in Daniel Berrigan's dialogue with the Nicaraguan priest-leader,

Ernesto Cardenal. In an *Open Letter* Berrigan responded to Cardenal who earlier had publicized his own decision to drop nonviolence and to take up armed resistance during the revolution against the Somoza regime.[46] Cardenal had given the best of reasons. His own people and village of Solentiname had been ruthlessly attacked. And the corruption of the Somoza regime was enough to allow any reasonable person to justify the revolution on the basis of just-war arguments. Yet Daniel Berrigan responded "no," a respectful and empathetic no, one filled with recognition of the institutional violence which Cardenal was up against. His no to Cardenal stemmed not from any simplistic ideology, but from a penetrating perception of Jesus' sermon as a long-range wisdom for Nicaragua. Berrigan saw then that the only way for Cardenal not to be "drawn into the dialectic" was to continue his path of nonviolence.

Berrigan's realist insight in that letter was not merely a poet's; rather it condensed the insight of a political scientist, an historian, an economist. He warned Cardenal that his struggle would never be limited to the Somoza regime, that it was also against interests even in the United States. In this we see how prophetic he was, as we have watched the United States take steps to isolate Nicaragua economically and politically, to destabilize the new government by violent attacks from guerrilla forces financed by the CIA, and as we have seen Nicaragua take steps of reaction and fear which surely will lead to its own inevitable militarization. This is precisely the inevitability which makes Berrigan's insight so profound. It is precisely what Pannikar meant by our being drawn into the dialectic, and the violence goes "on and on and on." Thus Panniker has pointed out for us something quite central, that nonviolence is not merely a doctrinaire following of Scripture or an ideology, but a practical long-range concern about effecting real change in human history.

Merton saw the power of this truth when he wrote about the witness of Gandhi. He points out how Westerners have tended too easily to create a myth. Though his words are almost caustic, they are important for our understanding of nonviolence:

> Sometimes the idea of nonviolence is taken to be the result of a purely sentimental evasion of unpleasant reality. Foggy cliches about Oriental metaphysics leave complacent Westerners with the idea that for the East (and as everyone knows, the Easterners are all "quietists" besides being "enigmatic") nothing really exists anyway. All is illusion, and suffering itself is illusion. Nonviolence becomes a way of "making violence stop" by sitting down in front of it and wishing it was not there. This, together with the refusal to eat meat or to kill ants, indeed, even mosquitos, is supposedly thought to create an aura of benevolence which may effectively inhibit the violence of Englishmen (who are in

any case kind to dogs, etc.) but cannot be expected to work against Nazis and Russians. So much for Western evaluations.[47]

I have quoted at length because the passage gives us an insight into more than Merton's use of sarcasm to puncture popular myths. He touches on a very important truth. Not only does he see Gandhi's nonviolence as eminently realistic in its concern for effecting historical change, but he also alludes to its actual potential for success even against ruthless dictatorships. This is a great value too of the Bishops' Pastoral, that for the first time they have explicitly recognized a form of pacifism which is clearly pragmatic, clearly even an aggressive strategy.[48] If certain sections of the Pastoral were really to be communicated to the grass roots, then American Catholics could begin to understand how a doctrine could develop, namely, how nonviolence seen as a strategic and assertive technique is the only way to authentic historical change.

The Bishops explicitly call attention to times when "there have been significant instances in which people have successfully resisted oppression without recourse to arms."[49] Their documentation for this point is especially important in that they refer to the studies of Dr. Gene Sharp, one of the most celebrated experts in the actual history of nonviolence and one who has documented its successful use precisely against dictators.[50] The Bishops are utterly concrete about this attempt of strategic nonviolence. They see it as needing to be "organized," as calling for "training," as requiring the "united will of a people" and as demanding "as much patience and sacrifice from those who practice it as is now demanded by war and preparation for war."

This is surely one more element of a development of doctrine. It is as though we are seeing the witness of the first three centuries put into a new light that enables us to read the history of pacifism without reading into it elements of passivity and meekness. Thus history has given us new material for the development of doctrine by which we can overcome an age-old dichotomy between love of self and love of enemy, between peace and justice, between the state's obligation and an individual's preference. In this sinful world we shall never overcome all the tension between these realities. But the Bishops have given us here a reflection which integrates the experience of Gandhi and of Martin Luther King, and out of it emerges a new theological vision of nonviolence. Thus they say that before we dismiss nonviolence as impractical or unrealistic, it must "be measured against the almost certain effects of a major war."[51]

This is genuine Christian realism. It is a view of nonviolence which is active not passive, historical and public rather than private and interior, assertive rather than surrendering, practical and pragmatic rather than pure other-worldliness. This is not to say that the pacifism of the Scriptures or of the early Christians lacked these qualities. Indeed, it may be that only through the gift of Gandhi do we begin to understand the full dimension of what took place in the early centuries. And is not this the customary way in the development of doctrine, that the "new" is of course a re-finding of the original doctrine in a new depth?

Conclusion

I end then where I began this essay. In our arguments over just-war teaching or nonviolence, we must try to get out of our heads and into the concrete world. And in that world we see the killing becoming unimaginably indiscriminate and brutal. In this real world we simply must try to stop so much evil; or we must at least diminish it. Grace calls us to lessen the violence of the killing; Christian realism begs us to stop the cycle of killing. But how can we ever even hope to stop the cycle in this real world? The times are urging upon us a realistic way, the way of nonviolence. In other words, the very impetus of the just-war teaching is pushing us to a development of doctrine which will finally teach a very simple word: no more violence, only nonviolence from here on, war no more. When will this time come? My own belief is that it is already upon us. It is now. It is already in the hearts of many. What remains is, I believe, simply a process of discernment amid a praying, suffering, loving Church, especially the Church of the little ones upon whom indiscriminate and unproportionate violence takes its first toll.

NOTES

1. Here I am using the term "Church of Nonviolence" rather than the term "Peace Church." There are so many differing theological emphases between the Roman Catholic tradition and some of the present Peace Churches; for example, a differing emphasis on the use of reason and a differing relationship with the human sciences and with the world in general. Any development of doctrine would have to be respectful of and in continuity with the unique gifts of the differing churches. For insightful critiques of the Catholic peace movement and the theologies of Church, see Charles Curran, "The Catholic Peace Movement and James W. Douglass," in his *American Catholic Social Ethics* (Notre Dame: Notre Dame Press, 1982), pp. 233–82.

2. Many have recognized a certain irony in Merton's refusal to be labeled a pacifist. See Gordon Zahn's Introduction to a work he edited: *Thomas Merton, the Nonviolent Alternative* (New York: Farrar, Straus, Giroux, 1980 edition); see pp. ix, xvii–xx.

3. See Rahner's study, *The Christian of the Future* (New York: Herder and Herder, 1967), pp. 39–48.

4. See the National Conference of Catholic Bishops' Resolution on Capital Punishment, November 1980.

5. Ruth Leger Sivard documents the progressive increase in civilian destruction in the wars of recent decades in her booklet, *World Military and Social Expenditures* (Leesburg, Va.: World Priorities, 1982), p. 15.

6. One notices that pacifists of our time often appeal to the destructiveness of modern war as part of the justification for their pacifism. The retort of the just-war theorist is that just-war teaching would also forbid such destruction. But the point here is that the pacifist, while not a methodological thinker, is in fact reaching for something deeper than mere logic. While Judith Dwyer criticizes pacifists, she does recognize that "the pacifists do not intend to write as ethicists." This she says in her unpublished dissertation, "An Analysis of Nuclear War in Light of the Traditional Just War Theory: An American Roman Catholic Perspective (1945-1981)," (The Catholic University of America, 1983), Vol. II, p. 447.

7. It was the quality of the weaponry—the brutal quality, that is—which Vatican II first looked at, and it was precisely from this examination that the Council issued its call that we undertake an "evaluation of war with an entirely new attitude." See *Pastoral Constitution on the Church in the Modern World*, no. 80.

8. *Loc. cit.*

9. For a brief explanation of the concept of Development of Doctrine, see Candido Pozo, "Development of Dogma," in Karl Rahner, ed., *Encyclopedia of Theology: The Concise Sacramentum Mundi* (New York: Seabury, 1975), pp. 356–60.

10. Many differentiate types and levels of pacifism. See, for example, Roland Bainton, *Christian Attitudes toward Peace and War* (Nashville: Abingdon, 1960), pp. 248–51; also 81–84.

11. Karl Rahner, "The Theology of Power," in *Theological Investigations,* Vol. IV (Baltimore: Helicon, 1966), p. 392.

12. National Conference of Catholic Bishops, *The Challenge of Peace: God's Promise and Our Response* (Washington, D.C.: United States Catholic Conference, 1983). See Section I C2, 74.

13. *Ibid.,* I, C4, 121.

14. Bryan Hehir makes reference to Pius XII's rejection of pacifism in his "Just-War Ethic and Catholic Theology . . . ," in Thomas Shannon, ed., *War or Peace: The Search for New Answers* (Maryknoll, N.Y.: Orbis, 1980), p. 17.

15. *The Pastoral Constitution on the Church in the Modern World*, no. 78.

16. The various parts of the Bishops' Pastoral in which there is a notable support for nonviolence are: I, C2, 73–74; I, C4, 111–21; III, A5, 221–30.

17. This is the basic argument in the public policy section of the Pastoral, namely, II B, 139–41 and II C, 142–61.

18. I owe this insightful caution to moral theologian Kenneth Hines, O.F.M., of the Washington Theological Union. He read this essay and gave critical suggestions for revision.

19. This phrase is the Bishops' own title for their section C on the just war and nonviolence. Previous drafts handled the relationship of the two subjects according to a different organizational framework.

20. NCCB, *Challenge of Peace*, I, C4, 120.

21. John Courtney Murray speaks of this development in his authoritative article introducing the *Declaration on Religious Freedom* in the Abbott and Gallagher edition of *The Documents of Vatican II* (New York: America Press, 1966), p. 673. Of

course, Murray's work had prepared the way for such a recognition of the development.

22. For a spiritual appreciation of the necessity of dealing with two things in tension, once could not do better than to call attention to the work of Simone Weil. See, for example, George Panichas, ed. *The Simone Weil Reader* (New York: McKay, 1977), pp. 345, 363–65.

23. Rahner brings out this point in the article cited in note 5, "The Theology of Power" p. 401.

24. Both David Hollenbach and James Childress mention several points touching on how nonviolence and just-war teaching have a complementary dimension. See Hollenbach, "Nuclear Weapons and Nuclear War: The Shape of the Catholic Debate," *Theological Studies* (December 1982), pp. 577–605. See especially pp. 580–87. Childress' article gave an especially helpful emphasis on the Christian presumption against the use of violence. See his article "Just War Theories," *Theological Studies* (September 1978), pp. 427–445. It may also be found in Thomas Shannon, ed., *War or Peace? The Search for New Answers* (Maryknoll, N.Y.: Orbis, 1980), pp. 40–58.

25. Rahner, *art. cit.*, pp. 393–95.

26. *Ibid.*, p. 393.

27. *Ibid.*, p. 398.

28. *Ibid.*, p. 393.

29. *Pastoral Constitution on the Church in the Modern World*, no. 79; also the Bishops' Pastoral, Section I, C2.

30. Joseph Komonchak, in a paper that is very receptive of the Bishops' Pastoral, critiques their section on Kingdom and History, indicating that there could be a greater appreciation of the Christological dimensions of the Kingdom, of the ethical force of the "already here" dimension of the Kingdom. *Catholics and Nuclear War: A Commentary on "The Challenge of Peace," the U.S. Catholic Bishops' Pastoral on War and Peace*, ed. Philip J. Murnion (New York: Crossroad, 1983) (Komonchak), pp. 106–116. The Bishops' theological reflections can be found most especially in Section I B.

31. Bernard Haring has made this a theme in his own work in the renewal of moral theology. See his *Free and Faithful in Christ*, Vol. I (New York: Seabury, 1978), p. 33, where he specifically speaks of Justin Martyr and the doctrine of the Fathers. See also John Paul II's *Redemptor Hominis*, where he specifically refers to the concept of the "Seeds of the Logos," no. II and footnote 67.

32. See John Paul II's General Audience Address of Feb. 21, 1979, where he speaks of the importance of naming injustices (*Origins,* March 8, 1979), p. 601.

33. *Art. cit.*, p. 395.

34. *Ibid.*, p. 395.

35. See Roland Bainton, *op. cit.,* pp. 91–95.

36. Bernard Haring has often called attention to the need to regain the eschatological tension in the renewal of moral theology. See, for example, *Free and Faithful in Christ,* Vol. I, pp. 56–58; 201–07; 209–10. Also see Charles Curran's "The Relevancy of the Ethical Teaching of Jesus," in his *A New Look at Christian Morality* (Notre Dame, Ind.: Fides, 1968), pp. 1–23.

37. H. Richard Niebuhr, *Christ and Culture* (New York: Harper and Row, 1951; Torchbook Edition, 1956), especially pp. 83–115, for his treatment of how the culture can absorb the Christ dimension of the Church.

38. I have tried to show how theologians carry responsibility in this matter and how at times our silence is not really a neutrality but rather a real acquiescence in the status quo of a militaristic build-up. "The Theologians' Role in Disarmament," *Proceedings of the Catholic Theological Society of America*, Vol. 37 (1982), pp. 148–54.

39. See James Douglass' point on how suffering is a witness which the nonviolent person brings to the issue of peace, in his *Nonviolent Cross* (New York: Macmillan, 1966), pp. 175–77.

40. Raimundo Pannikar, "The Myth of Pluralism: The Tower of Babel: A Meditation on Non-Violence," *Cross Currents*, 29 (Summer, 1979), pp. 197–230.

41. *Ibid.*, p. 218.

42. *Ibid.*, p. 221.

43. The concept of whether our ethics is deontologic as over against teleologic is a source of protracted controversy today. See, for example, Richard McCormick and Paul Ramsey, eds., *Doing Evil to Achieve Good* (Chicago: Loyola University Press, 1978). Here I am simply indicating that Jesus' commands have a human dimension, a wisdom dimension. That is, they are for our good. There is a slogan which has been used often in the effort to counter a nominalistic ethics: "That which is commanded is commanded because it is good; it is not good because it is commanded." Such is the case with nonviolence.

44. *Art. cit.*, p. 221.

45. *Ibid.*, p. 221.

46. See articles by both men: Ernesto Cardenal, "Solentiname Remembered," *National Catholic Reporter* (Feb. 3, 1978), pp. 11, 14; Daniel Berrigan, "Open Letter: Berrigan to Cardenal: Guns Don't Work," *National Catholic Reporter* (May 5, 1978), pp. 12, 18.

47. Thomas Merton, *Gandhi on Non-Violence* (New York: New Directions Press, 1965), p. 11.

48. NCCB, *Challenge of Peace*, III, A5, 221–30.

49. *Ibid.*, Section III, A5, 222.

50. Gene Sharp, *The Politics of Nonviolent Action*, 3 vols. (Boston: Porter Sargent Press, 1973).

51. NCCB, *Challenge of Peace*, III, A5 a, 223.